# FOUR STUDIES ON THE ECONOMIC DEVELOPMENT OF TURKEY

# FOUR STUDIES ON THE ECONOMIC DEVELOPMENT OF TURKEY

FREDERIC C. SHORTER
(*Co-Author and Editor*)
JOHN F. KOLARS
DANKWART A. RUSTOW
OKTAY YENAL

Routledge
Taylor & Francis Group
LONDON AND NEW YORK

First published 1967 by Routledge

2 Park Square, Milton Park, Abingdon, Oxon OX14 4RN
711 Third Avenue, New York, NY 10017, USA

*Routledge is an imprint of the Taylor & Francis Group, an informa business*

First issued in paperback 2016

Transferred to Digital Printing 2006



***This book is one of a series, Princeton Studies on the Near East***

ISBN 978-0-7146-1136-5 (hbk)
ISBN 978-1-138-97460-9 (pbk)

**Publisher's Note**
The publisher has gone to great lengths to ensure the quality of this reprint but points out that some imperfections in the original may be apparent

# CONTENTS

# LIST OF TABLES

# LIST OF DIAGRAMS AND MAP

# ACKNOWLEDGEMENTS

IT is a pleasure to acknowledge, on behalf of all the authors, the advice and encouragement which have been received from many quarters, and to note here the names of some of those professional friends and colleagues who assisted. The following read manuscript, participated in discussion, and helped in other ways: Morroe Berger, Lester V. Chandler, Sa'id El-Naggar, Frederick W. Frey, Manfred Halpern, Norman Itzkowitz, Kemal Karpat, Malcolm Kerr, Ann L. Kolars, James Land, Bernard Lewis, W. Arthur Lewis, Donald Mead, Osman Okyar, Gardner Patterson, Edith F. Penrose, William R. Polk, Richard D. Robinson, Lewis V. Thomas, Orhan Türkay, Walter F. Weiker, and Aysel Yenal. Certain others are bound by their institutional affiliations to remain anonymous, but they are also remembered with appreciation. The Program in Near Eastern Studies of Princeton University, which is directed by Morroe Berger, sponsored the weekly seminar and the concluding research conference at which the preliminary results of these studies were presented and criticized. The Program also defrayed expenses. Although each of us received generous assistance from these sources, we assume final responsibility for our respective chapters.

THE EDITOR

Princeton, New Jersey
*May* 1966

CHAPTER 1

# Introduction

*by Frederic C. Shorter*

THE traditional interpreters of Turkey to Western readers are the historians and orientalists who, together with occasional journalists, diplomats, and travellers, have built our images of the Ottoman Turks and of Republican Turkey. For an understanding of present-day Turkey, therefore, the traditional sources are central, but they no longer stand alone or even unchallenged. Today, scholars are bringing the perspectives and tools of economics, sociology, anthropology, politics, cultural geography, and other social disciplines to the study of Turkey. Their findings are broadening and deepening knowledge concerning Turkey's history and her present position. These contributions are an early indication of a forthcoming expansion of sources and methods of study which is already making new demands on both the consumers and producers of knowledge concerning contemporary Turkey.

The consumers of Turkish studies have long depended upon historians and orientalists to gather and interpret the significant social materials. In continuation of that tradition there is a vigorous school which insists that historians and orientalists have today, as earlier, both the responsibility and the capacity to present the "whole" society and its most essential themes. Theirs is a creative aspiration which remains valid as aspiration, and a few may succeed in fulfilling it to some degree. Meanwhile, however, consumers face the prospect that the rising volume of specialized materials will not all be read by the historians and orientalists, and if it is, may not all be understood or used well.

A sign of change in the role of the general interpreter of Turkish society is the avoidance of questions which are regarded as "too complex" or "difficult" for anyone except the specialists, for example economic questions. Such avoidance soon transforms the generalist into a specialist himself. The trend is explicable, and even justifiable as necessary, because producers should employ the best tools available for each subject. The time required to become and remain a skilled craftsman in all the relevant fields is more than one scholar has at his disposal. While specialization thus suits scholars as producers, it suits neither them nor other students of modern Turkey as consumers. As the latter, they have need to become literate in all the main subdivisions of social knowledge if they would understand Turkey well.

For the producers of Turkish studies their direct confrontation with a group of ultimate consumers should be a welcome, even if it is a disturbing, challenge in certain respects. It avoids having to speak first to the historians, and through them to the final consumers, which is fine when it works well, but which is more often than not restrictive of the flow of information and ideas. Unfortunately, many in the social disciplines are trained, and rewarded, for selecting and interpreting reality only as their respective disciplines see it. They do so within the discipline itself, where a high degree of technical literacy may be assumed and where a body of agreed interpretations already exists. Consequently, few have had experience in sharing their findings with those who see the same reality from a different perspective and who lack prior conditioning and training in the discipline. Still fewer have been satisfied by their experience with multi-disciplinary interchange.

The solution to this difficulty of communication is not for the producers of new works on Turkey to dilute, and thus to weaken, their methods of inquiry. It is up to the users of Turkish materials, especially when they are themselves scholars, to extend the range of their common intellectual experience. They can make the effort to understand and to appreciate both the perspectives and the findings of each other. It is an established psychological principle that shared experience while in the pursuit of common goals leads to an ability to perceive reality similarly. The eventual effect of such a convergence in perceptions should be an improved capacity of specialists to communicate findings to their consumers, because they will have a larger stock of common imagery to draw upon. For consumers and producers alike, therefore, direct confrontation in the pursuit of a full and deep knowledge of Turkey should be rewarding even though it requires much patience and diligence.

Accordingly, a confrontation among specialists on Turkey and Egypt took place at Princeton University in 1964. The group which gathered met regularly during a five-month period and exchanged the results of current research on economic development in Turkey and, although not directly related to this volume, on Egyptian development as well. Most of the relevant disciplines were represented. Selected topics were examined further in a research conference which reviewed the work at the end of the period and to which scholars from more distant locations were invited.

Even if the encounters between producers and consumers had gone no further, the attempts to communicate, to listen, and to understand would have rewarded those who attended sufficiently to justify the effort. Certain topics succeeded quickly. Others appeared to be excessively technical or obscure. Each had its advocates, which made it significant, if not as a report of new and important findings, then as representative of a perspective prevalent in one of the disciplines. In all cases the producers were induced to become more, rather than less, precise in handling materials because they found that they needed to know, and to say, exactly what they meant when addressing persons who came to the subject with assumptions different from their own.

The decision to publish four of the seminar's Turkish studies in one place, rather than as scattered contributions in journals of economics, politics, and geography, is a way of asserting that the present generation of contributors to Turkish studies aspires, in their capacity as readers, to an ability to range over materials which are diverse in their topics, points of view, and methods. The authors make the assumption that other users, like themselves, will welcome these contributions in order to help build their own understanding of Turkey's economic development. This book presents four studies having that end in view.

CHAPTER 2

# Politics and Development Policy

*by Dankwart A. Rustow*

THE political upheaval of 1960–61 has thrown Turkey into a condition of accelerated social change where politics and economics interact with redoubled intensity. Economic development is widely acknowledged as a goal and pursued with a new sense of urgency. For the last two decades, Turkey's population has been expanding faster than ever and flocking into the sprawling cities in unprecedented numbers. There is more social as well as geographic mobility. Group demands for economic advantage are being pressed with new vigour by businessmen, labour unions, and landowners. A greater variety of political ideologies is being advocated than ever before. Planning and social justice are principles invoked on all sides, but there is little agreement on the goals of planning or the standards of justice. Throughout the 1960s, economic issues have outclamoured most others in a continuous debate within the government, in the legislature, and before the electorate. But democracy and freedom of expression are themselves coming under attack. If at any future time ambitious colonels or doctrinaire professors should force democratic institutions into a sterner authoritarian mould, the requirements of economic development are likely to furnish the rationale, or at least a major pretext, for such a change.

The following pages will attempt to identify the economic attitudes and policies characteristic of major political and social groups and the impact that these groups are likely to have on economic policy and development.

## ELITE ATTITUDES: OTTOMANISM, KEMALISM, AND MODERNITY

The men who are responsible for the government of Turkey, including its economic policies, still are sufficiently homogeneous in background and outlook and sufficiently distinct from the rest of the population to be called a ruling élite. Turkey's rulers are city-dwellers and they are the products of a uniform state system of higher education. The older state universities of Istanbul and Ankara have in the past supplied virtually all positions in the country's administration. Graduates of the Ankara Faculty of Political

Sciences, successor of the Mülkiye (or Ottoman Civil Service School), fill most of the positions in the ministry of the interior with its centralized system of provincial and local administration. Many tax collectors and diplomats are products of this same Faculty. Law school graduates from Istanbul and Ankara serve as judges and prosecutors and as legal experts in the many public economic enterprises. Young men and women with diplomas from the Istanbul Faculty of Letters or the Ankara Faculty of Language, History, and Geography serve as secondary school teachers throughout the sixty-seven provinces. Only the military services have their own, separate hierarchy of schools including the Officers' School (Harbiye Mektebi) and the General Staff College (Harp Akademileri). In addition to the professional officers who emerge from these institutions, all male graduates of lycées (until 1960) and universities have been brought into close contact with the military system of education during their prescribed tours of duty as reserve officers.

The distinction between rulers and subjects in Turkey traditionally has rested on education. Just as a major branch of the Ottoman state machinery was the Imperial palace school, founded in the fifteenth century for the training of military and civilian officials, so the training of future public officials remains one of the major functions of government today. In theory, the state system of higher education for nearly a century has been open to any graduates of secondary schools throughout the country. Any peasant who can spare his son's labour in the fields and can put him through primary school (*ilk mektep* and *orta mektep*) and high school (*lise*, or lycée) may see him enter the university on a government scholarship and, on that basis, rise to the highest positions in society. In practice, such social ascent is severely restricted by rural poverty and by the shortage of schools. As late as the 1950s, fully half the students at the Faculty of Political Sciences were themselves the children of public servants.

Although Turkey still is far from universal education or complete social mobility, the age-old monopoly of the governmental élite has now at last been challenged. The change is most obvious in the composition of the legislative branch, the Grand National Assembly of Turkey. During the one-party system of the First Republic, from 1923 to 1946, from forty-six to fifty-four per cent of all assemblymen were government officials.[1] The transition to a competitive party system reduced the percentage of government officials to thirty-six in 1946, to twenty-two in 1950, and twenty-one in 1954. Although no comparable figures are available for the 1957–60 assembly or for the parliaments of the Second Republic elected since 1961, there is no doubt that the same trend continues. Lawyers, gentleman farmers, physicians, and businessmen in growing numbers have taken the legislative seats once reserved for civil servants, army officers, and teachers. The social pressures that have had such striking effect within the halls of parliament are felt if anything more strongly on the outside. The governmental élite no longer can rule the country in haughty isolation from the rest of the citizenry. The government's actions now are subject to close scrutiny by the press, to influence by chambers of commerce and labour unions, to demagogical attack by partisan orators, and to the ambiguous verdict of a peasant electorate. Conversely, where only a generation ago the state was almost the sole employer for the university graduate, there now are ample opportunities in business, in the press, in private legal and medical practice, and in other private careers to provide major competition. Whereas the educated and the ruling élite once were identical, the former now is much larger than the latter.

The ethos of the educated Turk reflects historic tradition as well as present pressure for change. The élite is heir to a continuous tradition of political responsibility that goes back to the beginnings of the Ottoman state in the thirteenth century. Although there have been profound changes in political institutions and in the recruitment of rulers, Turkey has never experienced such sudden discontinuities as colonial occupation or class revolution. In contrast to Egypt, for example, Turkey has never undergone the equivalent of Muhammad Ali's dispossession of Mamluk power, Cromer's establishment of a British administration in the Nile Valley, or even Nasir's social revolution unleashed from above.

The attitudes of the Turkish administrator and political leader therefore are likely to be a mixture, in proportions varying for each individual, of successive historic residues. The oldest of these is an Ottoman legacy. Any government official is a gentleman, a *bey*, a member of a ruling class, and to maintain that status he must conform to the manners of that class. Before he can govern others he must learn to govern his own passions and strive for moderation in word and deed. He disdains physical work, which is the lot of the lower social orders. Instead he must master the subtleties of refined speech; for the spoken word and a knowledge of human motives are the proper instruments of the true ruler. He takes pride not in his birth but in his upbringing. His social position is defined primarily by his service to the state, and it is from the state that he expects his economic rewards. In this Ottoman tradition social relations, like governmental affairs, are regulated by a sense of strict hierarchy, based on such visible factors as rank, age, and sex, and acknowledged by the use of different forms of speech to superiors and to inferiors. Any concerted activity requires a clearly recognized leader: there is no sense of group responsibility, let alone of anonymity in committee or council. The desire for power—for office, honour and wealth—is recognized as a universal human instinct. For a member of the ruling class, the pursuit of power is entirely honourable as long as he uses honourable means of service to the state, of deference to superiors, of personal and family connections. Family loyalty is the only restraint upon the individual's pursuit of power. In interpreting the actions of others, personal or family advantage therefore suggest themselves as ubiquitous motives. The proper business of the state in the Ottoman tradition is warfare and the training of future servants of the state; the maintenance of law and order and the collection of taxes are necessary adjuncts to these primary concerns. Economic production, however, whether in agriculture or in handicrafts, and trade are the specific pursuits of the subject classes and hence altogether unworthy of the ruler. The validity of this subtle and complex ethical structure is sanctioned by the truth of the Islamic revelation, whose staunchest defenders for over six hundred years the Ottomans were proud to be.

The second historical residue we may call the Kemalist legacy, even though it embraces many attitudes already developed in the Tanzimat and Young Turk periods. It contrasts sharply with the classical pre-Tanzimat Ottoman attitudes just described; yet it, too, has become historic—a legacy of education and memory rather than a response to current stimuli. The central aim of Kemalism was, in Atatürk's own words, "to make the Turkish nation attain the place that is its due within the civilized world".[2] The Kemalist is a nationalist and a modernizer. As a nationalist he acknowledges a common bond with other Turks of all social stations and holds Turkish virtue and strength to be superior to those of other peoples. While he has no desire to see Turks rule over others, he cherishes national independence as the supreme good. Hence military strength is important not for conquest as in Ottoman times, but for defence in a world of warring states. As a modernizer he admires the industrial civilization of the West and its values of scientific inquiry, of technical progress, of individual expression in the arts. He is a firm believer in the efficacy of education as an instrument of national unity and of liberating the peasant masses from ignorance and backwardness. The populism which is an article of the Kemalist creed implies government not by the people but for the people, at least until such time as education and reformist legislation shall have raised the people to requisite degrees of maturity and understanding. To the Kemalist, economic affairs are a proper preoccupation of the state, but here, too, the first imperative is independence from abroad. There must be no privileged position for foreign enterprises or for non-Muslim minorities. While Turkey should make full use of foreign technology and foreign experts, there should be no dependence on foreign capital. It is better that the economy develop more slowly from its own resources than that it develop faster in a state of foreign dependence. There must be no assertion of conflicting group interests or ideologies within the body politic. The mere suggestion that there are distinct social classes is, to the more thin-skinned Kemalists, a slur on national honour and a threat to national unity. Ideologies, moreover, are likely to be of foreign derivation and hence in conflict with a true nationalist spirit. The only group that the Kemalist regularly singles out for special attention is youth, for youth is the guardian of the Kemalist heritage, the present generation's pledge of a better future. Religion is to be respected as a matter of private conscience but should be conceded no influence on public life. Like most new nationalisms, Kemalism is ambivalent in its evaluation of the national self and of others. At times the Kemalist asserts that the Turks are already the world's foremost people and hence have nothing to learn from others: "We resemble ourselves" was a favourite Kemalist slogan, and the "National History Thesis" promoted by Atatürk in his declining years claimed Turkish–Central Asian origins for most achievements of human civilization. At other times, the Kemalist resolutely espouses the universal values of modern civilization ("The truest guide in life is science" is another of Kemal's maxims inscribed over one of the portals of Ankara University), and modestly recognizes what distance Turkey must yet cover in their attainment. Perhaps a third Kemalist motto, carved into a pedestal near one of Ankara's main intersections, best sums up this cluster of attitudes: "Turk, be proud, work, be confident!" The sequence of the triple admonition is significant. There must be pride to motivate hard work, and hard work to justify confidence.

There is an important difference between the two attitudes I have described. The Ottoman ethos stems from a view of man, of society, and of a man's place in it; the Kemalist creed culminates in a programme of public policy. National pride has replaced religious self-confidence, there is a new, outward-looking orientation, and the educational curriculum has been totally recast. But Ottomans and Kemalists agree on the high value of education as such, on the importance of military affairs and of leadership, and on the primacy of foreign over domestic policy. Hence Kemalist public policies could be grafted without too much difficulty on Ottoman rules of personal conduct. With the passage of time, the two legacies thus have blended.

The third component in the attitudes of the Turkish political élite is a contemporary response. It is harder to define than the two historic legacies, for it is less unified and as yet imperfectly crystallized. Yet the changes in attitude and outlook of the ruling class since the 1940s, and especially since 1960, are so striking that a description must be ventured. The new men of Turkish politics no longer need to be admonished to work hard. Work now has become a habit, for many even a compulsion; politics has turned into a rough, competitive game in which haughty indolence is headed for a quick fall. Whereas the Ottoman gentleman owed it to his dignity to meet his appointments with unhurried tardiness, the new men are likely to boast subtly how rushed and how busy they are. It no longer is a compliment, as it was a generation ago, to tell an old acquaintance "Praise to God, you have grown stout!" The activities that keep waistlines trim are, to be sure, of the most varied sort: the interminable rounds of negotiations of the Ankara politician, the harrying schedule of the stump orator, the organization drives of the union leader, the quick deals of the businessman, the inexorable deadline of the journalist, the midnight researches of the scholar, even the charity balls of the fashionable matron. In the first half of this century, military staff officers were almost the only Turks imbued with an austere sense of dedication and a sustained desire for achievement. Today some similar attitudes pervade all of the political-economic-social élite: Everywhere there is a new emphasis on punctuality and precision, on competence and reliability, on ingenuity and accomplishment. The members of this new élite may react to the older Kemalist slogans with embarrassment or amusement; but the emergence of this new type of man is a vindication of a century of Ottoman and Kemalist efforts at Westernizing reform.

The new scheme of values encourages expression of opinion and pursuit of material advantage both by individuals and by organized groups. Meanwhile, two decades of political campaigning have involved ever larger masses in the political process. From 1948 to 1962, furthermore, the gross national product has doubled and *per capita* income risen by thirty-seven per cent (both proportions calculated at constant prices). This widening of economic opportunities, has led to an even steeper rise in aspirations. On the political scene the rapid succession of three fundamentally different régimes in less than two years (May 1960 to October 1961) has sharpened the power instincts of all members and would-be members of the political élite: Menderes' personal rule with its blend of majoritarianism, acquisitiveness, and semi-religious appeals; the military junta of 1960–61 with its combination of drastic method and uncertain purpose; and the fragile coalitions of the Second Republic, partly protected and partly hemmed in by the Chief of the General Staff and the martial law commands in the major cities. "Governmental power in the last two decades has been wielded on behalf of a variety of social groups, and each of these has had its appetites whetted. Farmers will want more agricultural development and high prices; businessmen wish to retain their profits and to make the major investment decisions free from government regulation; workers demand guaranteed wages and job security; civil servants look back with nostalgia to the time when a parliament of Kaimakams was the country's unchallenged ruler. To those disillusioned with democracy, the press offers a variety of nostrums from Panturanism and Islamic fundamentalism to fellow-travelling socialism. Others are hoping for some future great man who, like Atatürk, will save the country from confusion and discontent."[3] Into this picture of uncertainty and tension the general election of 1965 has reintroduced the hope of synthesis and stability.

## Business: the New Turkish Entrepreneur

Three major interest groups—businessmen, labour, and farmers—not only influence economic policy through their pressure on or participation in government; they also affect the economy more directly through their productive functions. Something, therefore, must be said about each of these groups.

The emergence of a Turkish business class is a recent and remarkable phenomenon. The ethnic division of labour of Ottoman society assigned the crafts and trades mainly to non-Turks—Greeks, Armenians and Jews. In the nineteenth century these were reinforced by resident Europeans who thrived under the capitulations system and were known to Westerners as Levantines and to Turks as Sweet-Water Franks. Englishmen have been called a nation of shopkeepers; the Turks traditionally have been a nation of soldiers and rulers, of peasants and shepherds. The Tanzimat period brought a first government venture into economic enterprise in the form of the Agricultural Bank, and the Şirket-i Hayriye (or "Benevolent Company"), which from the late nineteenth century operated the Bosphorus ferries, and seems to have been one of the first joint stock companies formed by Muslim Turks. Yet private banking, the construction of railroads, tramways, telegraphs, gas mains—all these were undertaken by European interests. Under the Ottoman Public Debt Administration (1881–1914), foreigners even collected major parts of the revenue.

The decade from 1914 to 1923 brought a first shift from foreign to Turkish business. The capitulations were abrogated upon Turkey's entry into the World War.[4] The expulsion of Armenians from the Eastern provinces in 1915–16, and the peaceful exchange of population with Greece (1923 ff.), eliminated many of the traders and market farmers of the country. Military requisition and civilian shortages during a decade of war, and the needs of reconstruction afterward, involved the government in regulatory activity far beyond the traditional spheres of customs collection, taxation, and public works. A minister of food served in the cabinet in 1918–19 and one for reconstruction and resettlement in 1923–24; many other economic ministers have been added since. In the twenties and thirties, the government bought out the foreign-owned transport, utility, and mining companies. The punitive "capital levy" (*varlık vergisi*) of 1942 destroyed many remaining Christian and Jewish establishments in the wholesale and retail trade of Istanbul.

As non-Muslims left the country or were forced to liquidate, their places were taken by Muslim Turks. The years from 1914 to 1945 thus saw the rise for the first time in history of a Turkish business class. Since the economic history of this period has received little attention in the literature, a few individual examples may illustrate the trends at work.

When Mahmud Celâl (Bayar),[5] twenty-three year old son of a country-town mufti, joined the Deutsche Orient-Bank as manager of its Bursa branch in 1907, he must have been one of the first Turks to rise to such commercial prominence. Throughout Celâl's career, he combined economics with politics. That same year he joined the secret Society of Union and Progress, and after the 1908 revolution became chief of its Izmir section. In 1919 he organized the national resistance in the Izmir region and later became one of Mustafa Kemal's vigorous supporters in the Ankara Assembly. He served in various cabinet posts in the early twenties, and again as minister of economy from 1932 to 1937. Meanwhile, from 1924 to 1932, he was the first director-general of the İş Bankası, the first all-Turkish commercial bank founded privately by a number of politicians from Kemal's inner circle, which he developed into a major holding company. Serving as prime minister at the time of Atatürk's death,

Bayar was replaced shortly after İnönü's accession, was one of the few political figures to speak out against the 1942 "capital levy", and in 1945 became the founder of the Democratic Party which brought him to the Presidency of the Republic in 1950.

An older contemporary of Bayar's was Süreyya İlmen (1874–1955), son of one of Abdülhamid's war ministers, in whose shadow he became a general in his early thirties. Reduced in rank after 1908, he contributed to the development of military aviation in the First World War but eventually resigned his commission to found a textile factory in Istanbul. His prospering business enabled him to undertake other ventures, including Istanbul's largest movie theatre and a variety of philanthropies. Elected to the National Assembly in 1927, he joined in 1930 the short-lived Free Party whose programme he influenced in a free-trade direction. After two more decades of business, he stepped forward once again in 1949 as chairman of the "Soil, Real Property, and Free Enterprise Party" which, however, enrolled few followers. His business was taken over by his son, Atıf İlmen, for many years president of the Istanbul Chamber of Commerce and something of a figure in the local Republican People's Party politics.[6]

A man of a very different sort was Kara Kemal, Union and Progress party chief in Istanbul, and toward the end of the First World War Turkey's first minister of food. In 1916, in the midst of severe wartime shortages in the capital, the city council at Kemal's behest levied a surcharge of 2 to 3 para on each loaf of bread, thereby creating "a capital fund which enabled it to enter into other commercial ventures" handled through Kara Kemal's Tradesmen's Association. Later on he hit upon the even more lucrative scheme of a weekly treasury subsidy to the capital's bakeries.[7] After the Unionist débâcle of 1918 Kara Kemal disappeared from public view, but in 1923 he participated in attempts to revive the Union and Progress movement, and in 1926 he was involved in an assassination plot against Mustafa Kemal. That same year he lost his life as a fugitive from justice.

Süreyya İlmen and Kara Kemal at their opposite ends of the political and ethical spectrum were by no means isolated figures of their generation. Nuri Demirağ (1886–1957), factory owner in Istanbul, in 1945 founded the first opposition group that heralded the transition from a one-party to a multi-party system; in 1954 he joined the Assembly as a member of the Democratic Party. Salâhaddin Âdil Paşa (b. 1882), who had spent part of his military career buying weapons in Sweden, retired from the army after the war of independence and founded a metal works in Istanbul. In 1950 he was elected to the Assembly as a Democrat, but as an old critic of Mustafa Kemal resigned in protest against the passage of a law for the protection of Atatürk's memory. Nuri Kıllıgil (1890–1949), Enver Paşa's younger brother and a guerrilla leader in the First World War, later founded a munitions factory in Istanbul. Sapancalı Hakkı as a young lieutenant participated in Enver's audacious raid upon the Sublime Porte that established the Unionist wartime dictatorship, but unlike most of his associates retired from both army and politics. In 1928 his name reappears as owner of a dry-dock firm which received a major contract to repair the largest Turkish naval vessel, the cruiser *Yavuz*. The contract was signed by another ex-Unionist officer, minister of the navy İhsan (Eryavuz), and caused a major scandal that resulted in İhsan's impeachment.[8]

The careers just reviewed illustrate the close ties that linked Turkey's first generation of businessmen to the political élite. Party ascendancy in the state and growing state control of the economy allowed enterprising men to convert their political power into economic success. Even where political connections played no part in their rise, the first businessmen were of necessity recruited from other walks of life. Officers who retired early from the military services were especially prominent, for the officer corps by the end of the nineteenth century had become the most intensely Westernized class in Turkey. Even at this stage, two distinct patterns are apparent. Kara Kemal and Sapancalı Hakkı used their political connections to further their commercial interests, and Celâl Bayar through most of his combined political and business activity. Men like İlmen, Demirağ, and Âdil, by contrast, rose in the economic world when they were politically out of favour and entered the legislature at times of moderation or reversal of governmental course.

In the 1930s, Atatürk's Republican People's Party adopted an economic policy of étatism spelled out in successive four-year plans (1934, 1938). This new course was made possible by the restoration of tariff sovereignty after the five-year interval (1923–28) imposed by the Lausanne Treaty; it provided one possible answer to the effects of the Great Depression on a primary producing country—and one readily suggested by the example of single-party régimes in Russia, Italy, and Germany. The main principles followed were autarchy and tariff protection as well as state-sponsored industrialization particularly in such fields as metallurgy, textiles, and glass. These economic activities, undertaken through two major public holding companies (the Etibank for mining and electric power and the Sümerbank for manufacturing), added to the government's economic activities in public transport and utilities, in the state monopolies (tobacco, alcoholic beverages), and in the armaments industry. Etatism, in short, was a policy of state capitalism rather than of socialism. Instead of nationalizing existing enterprises, the government developed new industries; and it displayed no hostility to private enterprise as such.

The second generation of Turkish businessmen represent a further evolution. Where once there was a certain influx on the higher levels from the governmental into the economic élite, there now is large-scale direct recruitment into business. Large firms in recent years have been willing to secure the services of young university graduates even if this meant repaying the government for scholarships that otherwise would commit the young men to several years of state service. For military officers and civil servants in mid-career, moreover, employment in business now offers a realistic alternative; hence they are more likely to stand their ground in disagreements with superiors or with government policy. But the typical head of a large firm now is a graduate of a university, of Robert College, or of some foreign course of study who has worked his way up in business. There even are a few entirely self-made men of lower class origin without benefit of higher education; the most notable example being Vehbi Koç, today the head of Turkey's largest commercial-industrial complex.

Although family businesses still predominate, the number of joint stock companies is growing. Even aside from shareholding, enterprises like those headed by Koç and Kâzım Taşkent are far too large to be run on a family basis: they have become impersonal private bureaucracies. Although the size of the leading firms might give them easy access to political power, the new businessmen simply do not have the time to run for political office on the side. Business and politics each have developed into specialized, full-time careers. Taşkent resigned after only two years of service as a Democratic member of the National Assembly (1950–52); Koç has participated in RPP politics but never been elected to office.

Businessmen naturally continue to cultivate friendly connections with civil servants responsible for administering the government's many regulations that directly affect their firm—taxes, import licences, exchange regulations, building permits, public works contracts, etc. But in addition they now engage in a wide range of public service and public relations activities, and this often as a group rather than individually. When Menderes in the late fifties forbade government statisticians from publishing figures that might reflect adversely on the country's economic condition, the statistical publications of the Union of Chambers of Commerce and Industry became the most informative source on economic developments. Two private economic research organizations are currently active in Istanbul, one aided by the Ford Foundation and sponsored by a number of Turkish business and labour groups, the other an all-Turkish and all-business undertaking. Business philanthropy similarly is finding new channels beyond the traditional objects of Muslim charity such as orphanages, mosques, and fountains. The first visible symbol of this new trend was the Vehbi Koç dormitory at Ankara University erected in the early fifties. In short, businessmen have become more conscious of their power and responsibility as a group and, in an age of growing democratic participation, of the need to influence a wider mass audience.

## Labour: Strength through Organization

In contrast to big business, organized labour has in the past played a negligible role on the Turkish political and economic scene; but its power may be expected to rise sharply in the next five or ten years. Manufacturing developed only slowly in the larger urban centres after the First World War. As late as 1951 there were only some 10,000 industrial establishments employing more than ten workers, the average number of workers being thirty-four. (Ten years later, the number of enterprises had gone up to 37,000, but most of the new additions were of small size, so that the number of workers per establishment went down to 16[9].) Labour organization, moreover, was handicapped by powerful economic and political factors. Many workers to this day are only seasonal or temporary migrants from the village. Since levels of skill are low, the steady flow of rural migration to the cities threatens to wipe out any economic gains the industrial workers may have made. Legislation on labour matters came slowly and long remained paternalistic. Two draft labour bills were rejected in 1924 and 1932; a first Labour Code finally was adopted in 1936, followed by a series of further laws in 1945 and 1946 and the Trade Union Act of 1947.[10] The 1936 code required employers to negotiate with worker delegates, and the act of 1947 authorized the formation of trade unions. But the rights to strike, to automatic dues check-off, and to collective bargaining were granted only by a new Labour Code adopted in 1963. The older laws provided for minimum wages and maximum hours (forty per week in 1936), safety and health conditions, and severance pay according to seniority. But there were many loopholes. For example, agricultural workers, workers in establishments with less than ten employees, and workers in most public enterprises were excluded from the scope of the 1936 law. The generous severance pay provisions of the 1947 code, which took effect after a worker had been on the job for six months, were evaded by many employers through the simple device of laying off and rehiring the same work force every five and a half months.

Until 1946, any labour organization in the form of a union or political party was prohibited under the sweeping provisions of the Law of Associations. Even in the late forties, several workers' or socialist parties were closed on charges (not always substantiated) of being communist. Intermittently, the ruling political parties have wooed worker support. The Union-and-Progress dominated Ottoman House of Representatives of 1919 included Numan Usta, an Istanbul munitions worker, who after a period of exile in Malta also joined the Ankara Assembly. In 1931 the RPP included a number of workers on its list of deputies, including a Zonguldak coal miner, but these served mainly a decorative purpose in a bureaucratic legislature. In the 1950 campaign, the right to strike and collective bargaining became an election issue, and both major parties promised these rights to the workers. But the Democratic government showed no inclination to perform on its promise, and the trade unions contented themselves with polite, deferential reminders. In the 1954 election a trade union committee led by members of the journalists' union tried without much success to influence the selection of party candidates in selected districts; only a handful of union leaders appeared on any of the ballots. By the mid-1950s the Menderes government was doing its best to bring the Turkish Confederation of Trade Unions under DP influence and did secure the election of a pliable Confederation chairman. In the late fifties the workers were under much pressure to join such DP ventures as the Cyprus-Is-Turkish Association and the Patriotic Front; they received few tangible rewards.

After the 1960 revolution, public attitudes were more favourable to labour demands. The workers themselves, moreover, no longer were relying on the old hat-in-hand approach to government and employers. One of the largest outdoor rallies ever held in Turkey demanded the fulfilment of long-standing promises for collective bargaining legislation, and a few strikes were called in specialized industries where neither government nor employers were inclined to invoke existing punitive legislation. The 1963 Code, which resulted in part from this pressure, already is causing a spurt in membership enrolment and consolidation among rival unions—for a union supported by fifty-one per cent of the work force of a single enterprise, or in an entire work branch in a given region or the country as a whole, now is entitled to bargain collectively for all workers in the given category. A few of the union leaders are lending their political support to left-wing intellectual undertakings, such as the Turkish Workers' party and the journal *Sosyal Adalet* (*Social Justice*). Many of the larger unions, notably the textile workers and the hotel and restaurant workers, are determined to hold aloof from partisanship. They fear that endorsement of this or that party by individual labour leaders will only serve to weaken the unions by introducing partisan squabbles into the organization, and conclude that time is not yet ripe for a working-class party. Instead they concentrate on organizational efforts which in turn will enable the unions to influence the major parties in accordance with the time-hallowed American Federation of Labour maxim of rewarding your friends and punishing your enemies. In the long run, the new Labour Code is sure to give a substantial boost to labour's reward-and-punishment power; in districts such as Istanbul, Ankara, Zonguldak, Eskisehir, and Adana a labour bloc-vote may well turn out to be an important factor in the foreseeable future.

A development of special interest is the growing number of Turkish workers going to Germany and other West European countries for one or two years of work in the mines or on the assembly line. At the end of 1965 there were over 150,000 of these workers—not a large number within the German total but equivalent to more than one worker in ten in the Turkish industrial labour force. Even more significant, perhaps, is the fact that 750,000 more registered with the official labour exchange to take their turns. The remittances of the workers ($100 million was the total anticipated for 1966) are a major boon to the foreign exchange balance. Just what the social and political consequences of this labour migration will be for Turkey depends largely on how the programme is handled. Is the workers' experience in Germany and elsewhere such as to make them more friendly or hostile to the West? Upon their return will they be reintegrated into the industrial work force or will they be tempted to become marginal entrepreneurs—taxi-drivers, shopkeepers, etc.—prone to early bankruptcy and disillusionment? In any case, direct contact with Europe, for over a century a precious privilege of the intellectual, for the first time is becoming part of the experience of the manual worker.[11]

## The Farmers: Local Divisions and National Power

Farming employs nearly two-thirds of the Turkish population, but throughout most of history the Anatolian farmer has taken no active part in public affairs beyond his village. In early Ottoman times recruiting agents would periodically round up boys from the Christian villages for service in army or government under the so-called *devşirme* system. In the eighteenth century this practice lapsed, and since the nineteenth Muslim peasant boys have instead been drafted into the army. Other government agents would collect the tithe or later the land tax. But, apart from military recruitment and taxation, the government took as little notice of the villager as the villager did of the government. Politics was an exclusive concern of the cities, of the sultan and his ministers in Istanbul, of the governor or the judge in the provincial town. The War of Independence showed that the ultimate defence of Anatolia depended on its peasant population, and during the Kemalist one-party period the government paid some sporadic attention to agricultural problems. Atatürk, in a much-quoted saying, stated that the villager was the real owner of the country, and a model farm near Ankara was one of his favourite leisure-time preoccupations. More consistently, the government expanded the system of primary education, nearly quadrupling the rate of literacy in two decades (6·0 per cent in 1927 to 23·4 per cent in 1945). The school teacher thus joined the tax collector, the conscription officer, and the imam as a connecting link between the village and the rest of society.

A basic change in relations between city and village came about with the advent of competitive parties in the late nineteen-forties. For the first time the rural majority was given a decisive voice in choosing the country's rulers. As a result, city politicians appeared on the village squares at shorter and shorter intervals, not to give curt orders to the sullen peasantry, but rather to learn about the peasants' complaints and grievances and to sway his vote in favour of this party or that. The RPP supplemented its network of People's Houses in the cities with People's Rooms in the villages. Competing with intensive opposition activity, the RPP founded more local branches in the years from 1946 to 1950 than it had in the preceding quarter-century.

The heavy turnouts of villagers at the polls amply rewarded the politicians' solicitude: in the first free elections in 1950 and 1954 nearly ninety per cent of all Turkish adults used the ballot, and when voter interest declined slightly in 1957 the drop came mainly in the urban rather than the rural constituencies. The political shift from a government elected by the urban educated class to a government elected by the peasant majority had striking consequences. Where once economic policy had emphasized industrialization only, there now was systematic attention to rural needs: support prices for wheat, feeder roads to link villages to outside markets, dams for irrigation as well as electricity, water wells, rural school houses, and village mosques. In deference to the peasantry's conservatism, both major parties, moreover, concurred to limit the radical secularism of the Kemalist period. Significantly, the only resounding legislative defeat suffered by the Menderes government in ten years was on a proposal to increase the land tax. Since a tenfold increase had been demanded there is some question as to government's sincerity; but the legislators' vote in any case reflected the new power wielded by the rural majority.

Although the peasants participate in elections, the candidates whom they elect still are gentlemen of the élite. In the Assembly there has been a shift, as we have seen, from bureaucrats to lawyers, landowners, and merchants, but no peasant has yet run for national political office.

Some statistical indicators of relative rural prosperity reveal the cumulative effect of fifteen years of rural development. In 1960, 83·2 per cent of all peasants lived in villages with a mosque, 74·2 per cent had access to the outside world by a road passable by motor vehicle (that is, presumably, at least a jeep with four-wheel drive), 72·7 per cent had a primary school in their village, 43·9 per cent a coffee house, 36·0 per cent piped water (from well or surface conduit), and 23·9 per cent at least one telephone in the village.[12]

The new political power of the villagers magnifies the importance of economic and social divisions among the rural population—a subject that still has received too little attention from government statisticians and academic researchers. We know that in 1950 94·1 per cent of all Turkish farm families owned at least some of their land, and 72·6 per cent all of it. In contrast to the traditional situation in Iran, Iraq and Syria, where a narrow class of large landowners has ruled a population of tenants or farm labourers, Turkey has traditionally been a country of peasant-owners. But if the size of holdings and productivity of the land are taken into account, the picture shifts considerably. In 1950, 0·8 per cent of all rural families owned 19·6 per cent of the cultivated area, with half the total agricultural land in the hands of only 9·3 per cent of the families.[13]

These data confirm what is known from recent Turkish history about the persistent influence of prominent provincial families. The frequency with which certain names recur in parliamentary delegations and on lists of other political leaders of a given province from

Ottoman times to the present is striking—the Cenanis in Ayıntab, the Mardinizades in Mardin, the Princcizades in Diyarbakır, the Mursaloğlus in the Hatay, the Ramazanoğlus in İçel, the Karaosmanoğlus in Manisa, the Menemenlizades (Menemencioğlus) near Adana, and many others. Some of these are descended from old *ulema* families (e.g. Mardinizade), some even claim descent from the Prophet (e.g. Cenani), some are old *âyan* families (i.e. provincial notables whose hereditary power was broken by Mahmud II—e.g. Karaosmanoğlu), some are descended from the chiefs of nomadic tribes (Türkmen—e.g. Menemencioğlu, or Kurdish—e.g. Babanzade). Usually these families reside in the provincial town or in Istanbul and now Ankara, but their wealth and influence continue to be based on substantial land holdings. They may be prominent in various political parties, but they do not owe their position to political organization; rather, successive political parties court them and derive regional strength from their support. To cite a single striking example, Selim Seven, a Kurdish tribal chief in Hakkâri, ran unopposed as an RPP candidate in 1946 and 1950 (the second time his was the only uncontested district in the country); in 1952 he joined the DP, and in 1954 and 1957 his son Übeydullah received more than two-thirds of the Hakkâri vote on a DP ticket.

Broadly, therefore, we can distinguish at least three rural strata. First, there are the large estate owners who can send their sons to high school, university, and foreign study and who over the decades or centuries have become an integral part of the political élite. Then there is an even larger class of owners of large tracts of farmland who sell their produce in the market, easily make the transition from farming to commerce, and rose to prominence in provincial and national politics in the 1950s. Finally, there is the large mass of subsistence farmers, sharecroppers, and farm labourers who still play no political role except as voters.

But there are divisions within the rural population other than those marked by wealth and size of land holdings. Turkey has more ethnic and religious homogeneity than most countries of Asia and Africa: ninety-nine per cent of the population are Muslims and ninety-three per cent speak Turkish as their mother tongue.[14] In some regions, however, the non-Turkish groups are of great importance. In eight south-eastern vilâyets, Kurds outnumber Turks, in eight other eastern provinces they form from eleven to forty-nine per cent of the population; thirty-six per cent of the Hatay population are Arabs; in Artvin, thirteen per cent of the population are Lazes or Georgians; and in urban Istanbul, non-Muslims (Greeks,

Armenians, Jews) constitute eleven per cent. Equally significant in regional politics are other groups who are Muslim in religion and often Turkish in language but sufficiently distinct in their culture to retain some separate identity. These include the Türkmen nomads of the Taurus region—descended from the first Central Asian migrants to Anatolia—and many Muslim groups who in the last century found refuge in the Ottoman Empire: Circassians and other Caucasian Muslims, mainly in north-east Anatolia; Crimean Tatars; Turks who arrived under the population exchange with Greece in the twenties; and refugees from Bulgaria and from as far away as Sinkiang arriving in the 1950s. Even more important than these distinctions of geographic origin is a religious distinction among Muslim Turks, that between Sunnis and Alevis. Ottoman-Kemalist ideology, which draws a clear line between Muslim Turks and non-Muslim minorities, such as Greeks and Armenians, refuses to admit any group distinctions within the Muslim majority. As a result census data are scanty or biased. Alevis, in particular, have never been counted by census takers or anyone else, and guesses as to their total proportion in the population range wildly from five to thirty-five per cent.

But the practical politician whose election may hinge on a few thousand votes is apt to acknowledge social realities regardless of official ideology. As the example of Selim Seven indicates, all parties are likely to curry favour with the Kurdish social hierarchy in the eastern provinces, although the DP and more recently the New Turkey Party seem to have established the closest connection. In Sakarya province, a Circassian-descended candidate, such as the New Turkey Party leader Ekrem Alican, is an asset to an election list. In Istanbul the major parties have regularly put one Greek, one Armenian, and one Jew on their tickets.[15] In Urfa and Hatay some Arab candidates are indispensable. The province of Kırşehir, which includes the shrine of Hacı Bektaş, has long been the main stronghold of the Nation Party. Throughout Anatolia, party politicians take it for granted that the RPP's secularism holds a strong attraction for Alevi communities, who see in a strict separation of religion from politics the best guarantee against Sunni oppression. It would appear, therefore, that within the country's fundamental Muslim-Turkish homogeneity, there is a subtle chequerboard pattern of differences that crucially affects local political alignments, and on that basis national politics as well.

## The Political Brokers: Parties and Juntas

It would be convenient if the ideological, economic, and cultural differences just surveyed could be clearly correlated with alternative economic policies. But the connection is not that simple. Elections are won, cabinets formed, and policies adopted not by Ottoman-style gentlemen, modernizing nationalists, or hard-working technicians *as such*—nor by businessmen, trade unionists, peasants, Türkmen nomads, Kurds, Alevis, or Circassians acting *as groups*. It is political parties that name candidates and win elections, elected party politicians who enter the cabinet, and party leaders who formulate policies. Economic interests and social groups are the building blocs from which candidates put together local support, and parties are merely national confederations of such candidates. Once in office the elected politician faces an array of pressures quite different from those confronting the candidate—pressures as contradictory and as uncontrollable as the size of the Turkish wheat harvest, Kremlin pronouncements on Middle Eastern affairs, international demand for chromium and manganese, foreign aid appropriations in the United States Congress, and militant actions by the Greek community on Cyprus. Between the groups and interests that form his constituency and the outside realities with which policy must cope, the politician acts as a mediator or, if you will, as a broker. The constituent groups can be analysed, as we have done, and so can the policy alternatives, as we shall briefly attempt in the concluding section of this paper. But which particular policies a politician will "buy" and to what group of supporters he will "sell" these—what specific brokerage deals, in short, he will consummate—is much harder to predict.

I have suggested in another context that Turkish villages and small towns tend to divide into dual factions based on social, cultural, or economic differences—into what anthropologists call "moieties" —and "that the two major Turkish parties are nation-wide coalitions of such moieties, the local faction that was dominant in 1945 being the natural supporter of the RPP, its rival of the DP" or today of the Justice Party.[16] Be that as it may, the major Turkish parties certainly are not now ideological parties (whatever contrary impressions their programmes may convey) and just as certainly not nationwide class parties. Rather, all parties have clienteles representing widely overlapping social spectra, and their policies have a wide range of flexibility in response to many shifting circumstances.

This width and flexibility became apparent as soon as Turkey made the transition to a multi-party system. The Democratic Party was founded early in 1946, formulated its official programme, and soon took off on an impressive campaign of stump oratory which after four years carried it triumphantly into office. The DP chairman,

Celâl Bayar, had been one of İnönü's few possible rivals for the presidency in 1938, and many of his associates had similarly been thwarted in their ambitions. In its programme, the new party predictably endorsed those five principles of Kemalism that had come to be considered sacrosanct, concentrating its fire on the sixth, étatism, by promising a shift to liberal free enterprise. As they established contact with the conservative rural voters, the Democratic campaigners, again quite predictably, promised agricultural development and a retrenchment of secularism. Once in office, the DP gave its voters what it had promised: the Arabic prayer call, water wells, feeder roads, a high wheat support price, and new mosques. In short, composition of leadership, programme pronouncements, and campaign promises of government policy each evolved logically, but they followed each its distinct logic. Bayar, whose party programme promised free enterprise, had been minister of economics in the heyday of étatism; in any case, the ratio of public to private investment in a decade of DP rule remained nearly unchanged, although there was a shift in public investment from manufacturing to "infrastructure". Menderes, who was to become the idol of millions of small peasants, was a large landowner, and the four DP founders had first banded together in 1945 to oppose an RPP land distribution bill. Fuad Köprülü, another DP co-founder and key minister in the new cabinet which hastened to restore the Arabic prayer call, had been chairman of a commission in 1928 that recommended the translation into Turkish not just of the prayer call but of the entire Muslim liturgy.[17]

It may here be interjected that whatever the antecedents of the DP founders and whatever the wording of their programme, at least there was a close connection between campaign promises and performance in office. But it is doubtful whether an RPP administration in the 1950s would have carried out fundamentally different policies. In the late 1940s the RPP had already caught a bad case of me-too-ism on the religious issue and by 1950 had indeed anticipated many of the Democrats' demands (such as religious lessons in the schools, reopening of the Muslim mausoleums and other shrines, and foreign exchange allocations for Mecca pilgrims). And the pressure for greater agricultural development would probably have proven irresistible for any elected government. Yet the DP in 1950 was not merely a party of rural interests: it had the enthusiastic support of the business and professional community, including the non-Muslims of Istanbul, it had the strong sympathies of higher civil servants and other members of the traditional ruling élite, and the workers in many industrial communities remained faithful to it throughout the fifties. Nor were the DP's policies fixed for all time. On the religious issue, in particular, there were several reversals of direction: toward greater secularism in 1953–54 when religious agitation seemed to get out of hand; and back to religious appeals (implying that Menderes was God's chosen instrument for the Turks' salvation on earth) when the economic situation sharply deteriorated in the late 1950s.

Whatever the shifts and overlaps in party policies, the instability of party personnel is, if anything, more striking. Membership in the parliamentary parties is somewhat volatile. Opposition groups lose members through defection, government parties through expulsion. For example, of the fifty-nine DP members elected in 1946, twenty-four had left the party within two years; of the sixty-nine RPP members who took their seats in 1950, twelve had resigned by 1951; in 1954, the RPP's first defector was its floor leader. While some of the dissidents have formed splinter groups (e.g. the Nation Party 1948–49, the Peasant Party 1953, and the Freedom Party 1956, all offshoots from the Democrats), others have joined the opposite major party. Menderes liked to take RPP defectors into his cabinet since he found them more dependent on his favour than old DP members and hence a better buttress to his personal power. But the RPP has been almost as hospitable to converts; some of its present leaders, such as Fethi Çelikbaş, and Cihad Baban, had been staunch Democrats in the early fifties. Politicians of national repute and local favourite sons can carry out several switches of party without damage to their careers. But even among lesser figures there are few recorded cases when earlier enmity has prevented later admission to a given party. (Shifts from the Democratic Party, after its forcible dissolution in 1960, to the Justice and New Turkey Parties, newly founded in 1961, are not pertinent in this context; for the membership and the campaign appeals of these new groups clearly revealed their intention of providing a haven for orphaned DP voters.)

This section has so far dealt only with political parties. But there is another group that since 1960 has played a major role in politics, namely the military officers; and it might be thought that their specialized training, their strong group ethos, and their common professional experience would mould the officers into a distinct political group with clear-cut policies. But the experience of the last few years shows, on the contrary, that military officers quickly lose their sense of unity and direction after taking the first steps on the slippery political stage. At least three military groups must be distinguished within the recent Turkish context. One group of officers ruled the country as the National Unity Committee in 1960–61, and subsequently its members served as President of the Republic and as lifetime senators. A second group, in the general staff and other high command positions, has been acting on the political backstage at times as mediators among the feuding civilian parties, at times as their protectors from further military coups, and occasionally as a forceful pressure group on specific political issues. A third group in the last few years has been jailed, or relegated to the sidelines, as a result of various ill-starred attempts to seize power. (There may be a fourth group, those still in the armed forces who may be preparing a future coup, and naturally such a group would be careful not to broadcast its presence. It seems more likely, however, that would-be plotters will have been sufficiently warned by the failure of the third group to give up any early political ambitions.) Far from being a solid group with a single-minded purpose, it would seem that the military, as a result of nearly four decades of isolation from politics, had by 1960 become even more unsure and divided in their political responses than the civilian leaders. The thirty-seven officers who assumed power that year were united only in overthrowing and later executing Menderes; they also were generous in their appropriations to the armed forces, tried without full success to secure their position against challenge from officers on active duty, and tackled matters of economic and social policy with impatience and at times with imagination. But on basic political issues they were soon sharply divided. A minority of the junta, led by Alparslan Türkeş, wanted to perpetuate authoritarian government and institute a drastic, if somewhat naïve, social reform programme from above. The majority under Cemal Gürsel resolved on a speedy return to civilian democratic government and on a more moderate reform policy in the meantime. Periodic expulsions from the armed forces since 1961 and the evidence of the Aydemir trial of 1963 indicate to what extent personal rivalries have exacerbated feelings and complicated political action both within the moderate and within the radical group.[18]

## The Prospect Ahead

This brief examination of the forces on the Turkish political stage might suggest that the competing parties are all but indistinguishable in their sources of support, their personnel, and their policies; that they are (as the cynical saying used to go about parties in the United States) "like a red bottle with a blue label and a blue bottle with a red label, both empty"; that the background presence of the military introduces a capricious motif into an already confused picture; and that no intelligent estimate therefore can be made of the economic and social policies that Turkish governments are likely to adopt over the next decade.

Such scepticism, I suggest, would be excessive. The basic issues that now confront Turkish leaders and that are likely to plague their immediate successors can be identified with some assurance. And each of these issues allows only a limited number of responses, among which some will be more congenial to certain types of government and some to others.

There will be continued and perhaps mounting pressure for government action to promote economic development, for only in an expanding economy can the clamour for material advantage raised by organized groups in labour, business, and farming be satisfied. In view of the current reduction in America's world-wide aid programme, there is sure to be a continuing search for alternative sources, such as the Organization for Economic Co-operation and Development and the Soviet Union. While the Cyprus conflict continues, there is likely to be an arms race, mainly air and naval, with Greece and the Greek government on Cyprus. In the long run, internal pressures, a further lessening of American–Russian tensions, and disappointment with lack of Western support for Turkey's position on Cyprus may lead to a retrenchment of NATO commitments and to a limitation of military expenditures. The closer ties recently agreed upon with the Common Market conform to the ruling élite's deep conviction that Turkey is (or must become) an integral part of Europe; they also open the prospect of further economic aid from Europe—tied in with a heavy obligation upon Turkey to help itself so as to justify help from others. Such a pro-European course may be endangered, however, if the Cyprus question or an economic downswing should create a xenophobic mood in the electorate which press and opposition could readily exploit.

Whatever the prospects of outside economic assistance, there are sure to be pressures, from abroad and from inside Turkey, for additional *internal* financing of development. Such pressure is sure to sharpen conflicts over various social and economic reform proposals. New internal financing can come from heavier taxes, which must be apportioned among industrialists, salary and wage earners, landowners and farmers. Or it may be provided by inflation, which shifts the burden to the consumer, particularly government employees and others on fixed income. The uneven distribution of property in the country is sure to provide a continuing target for attack—either as now from radical intellectuals and reform-minded civil servants or perhaps in the future from industrial workers and the poorer peasants as well. But larger press circulation and better group organization will enable the privileged interests to fight back harder than in the past. There will be more clamorous demands for expanded education (this pressure already is coming from the villages and not just from urban intellectuals); hence there may be renewed conflict over secularism versus religious conservatism in the schools. Above all, the heavy rates of population growth and of urbanization will provide continued pressure for economic progress and social reform. The Turks these days must work hard to maintain current levels of employment and consumption and all the harder to improve them and bring them more nearly in line with Europe.

The 1965 elections have shown the remarkable resilience of Turkey's two-party system. As a result of the military intervention of 1960–61, Menderes had been executed, the Democratic Party banned, and some four hundred of its leaders barred from political participation. Only four years later, the Justice Party, which proudly assumed the succession to Menderes and the Democratic Party, swept into office with one of the largest pluralities in Turkish electoral history. But the cry for revenge that dominated the Justice Party's earlier propaganda had subsided. Its new leader, Süleyman Demirel, represented the moderate wing; by training he was an engineer, who had prominently participated in the development work of the 1950s, rather than a politician. Demirel's premiership thus represented the advent to power of the third, post-Ottoman and post-Kemalist generation of modernized Turkish leaders. It also marked a reconciliation of the earlier enmities between military and ex-Democrats, and hence made possible a more complete withdrawal of the military from the political stage.

The defeat of the RPP, reduced to only twenty-nine per cent of the popular vote, and the prospective retirement of its octogenarian leader has already brought to the fore many latent cleavages—notably the division between regional landowning interests that have long dominated many of the party's local organizations and a group of more ideologically inclined politicians who wish to transform the party into a Turkish equivalent of the British Labour Party. Although radical elements outside the major parties remained highly vocal, the 1965 election once again showed how little appeal they have to the average voter. The far-left Turkish Labour Party won only three per cent of the vote, and the Republican Peasants' Nation Party, led by the authoritarian ex-colonel Alparslan Türkeş, only two per cent.

Barring some unforeseen event that would interrupt the continuity of electoral politics in the Second Republic, the choice in Turkey was likely to remain one between Justice Party and Republican People's Party or their successors.

## NOTES

1. Including civil servants, military officers, and university and school teachers; if such marginal categories as physicians at government dispensaries and managers of government economic enterprises are added to these, it appears that well over half of all legislators were recruited from the public service. For detailed figures see Frederick W. Frey, *The Turkish Political Elite*, Cambridge, Mass., 1965, passim.
2. Atatürk, *Nutuk*, 1927, second last paragraph.
3. D. A. Rustow, "Turkey's Second Try at Democracy", *The Yale Review*, Vol. 52, No. 4, Summer 1963, pp. 535 f. The "Parliament of Kaimakams" echoes a satirical comment by Sir Mark Sykes who, travelling through Eastern Turkey toward the turn of the century, saw this as the ideal of the half-Westernized Ottoman administrator. See Robert E. Ward and D. A. Rustow, eds., *Political Modernization in Japan and Turkey*, Princeton, 1964, p. 115.
4. For text of the decree see J. C. Hurewitz, *Diplomacy in the Near and Middle East*, Princeton, 1956, ii, 2–3.
5. Names in parentheses are family names adopted under the law of 1934. On the development of the Turkish business class cf. Alec P. Alexander, "Industrial Entrepreneurship in Turkey: Origins and Growth", *Economic Development and Cultural Change*, Vol. 8, pp. 349–65.
6. On İlmen see his memoirs in several volumes (Vol. 3, entitled *Dört ay yaşamış olan zavallı Serbest Fırka*, was published in Istanbul in 1951), and İbrahim Alaettin Gövsa, *Türk meşhurları ansikopedisi*, Istanbul (1946), pp. 363 f.
7. The quote is from the unblushing annual report of the Society of Union and Progress for 1916 [German translation in *Korrespondenzblatt der Nachrichtenstelle für den Orient*, Vol. iii, No. 2 (21 October 1916), Supplement]. Cf. Ahmed Emin (Yalman), *Turkey in the World War*, New Haven, 1930, pp. 125 and 133.
8. On Eryavuz see the biographical sketch by Samet Ağaoğlu in his *Babamın arkadaşları*, Istanbul (1959), pp. 44–61; on the connection with Hakkı esp. p. 50. On Kıllıgil, *ibid.*, pp. 30–4, and my article "Enver Pasha", *Encyclopaedia of Islam*, 2nd edn., ii, 701 f. Note İhsan's unrepentant choice of last name six years after the scandal.
9. İşçi Sıgortalari Kurumu Umum Müdürlüğü, *İsci sigortaları kurumu 1961 iş ve faaliyet istatistikleri*, Ankara, 1962.
10. Zvi Yehuda Hershlag, *Turkey: An Economy in Transition*, The Hague (1958), pp. 288 ff.
11. See further Nermin Abadan, *Batı Almanyadaki Türk İşçileri ve Sorunları*, Ankara, 1964.
12. See State Institute of Statistics, *Statistics of Village Characteristics 1960 Survey Results*, Ankara 1963, passim. In all categories there was a small percentage of "unknowns" (ranging from 0·4 per cent for imams to 2·4 per cent for roads); I have assumed that in these villages the respective facility was not available.
13. See the results of the 1950 census of agriculture (Central Statistical Office, *Statistical Résumés*, No. 12/s:1, Ankara 1953, pp. 8 and 11). Estimates by Eva Hirsch of distribution of agricultural *income* from operation of land owned or rented plus seasonal wages generally agree with the figures for distribution of *land ownership*. She calculates that the poorest ten per cent of the rural population (including landless workers) received 1·38 per cent, the poorest twenty per cent of the population 3·27 per cent of the income. See her unpublished Ph.D. thesis, *Income Distribution in Turkish Agriculture*, Columbia University, 1960, p. 188.
14. According to the official statistics for 1955, based on a ten per cent sample.

15. Under the party-list plurality system of the 1950s this assured them of one seat apiece among the thirty-odd Istanbul deputies in parliament. Under the proportional system of the Second Republic the non-Muslims, being far down on each party's list of candidates, stand little chance of election.

16. See my essay on "Political Parties and Ruling Elites in Turkey", in Joseph LaPalombara and Myron Weiner (eds.), *Political Parties and Political Development*, Princeton, 1966, p. 123.

17. For further details see my chapter on "Politics and Islam in Turkey, 1920–1955," in Richard N. Frye (ed.), *Islam and the West*, The Hague, 1957, p. 83.

18. On the military in recent politics see Walter F. Weiker, *The Turkish Revolution 1960–1961: Aspects of Military Politics*, Washington, D.C., 1963; and idem, "The Aydemir Case and Turkey's Political Dilemma", *Middle Eastern Affairs*, Vol. XIV, pp. 258–71 (November 1963).

CHAPTER 3

# Military Expenditures and the Allocation of Resources

*by Frederic C. Shorter*

AN important element of most strategies of development is to depress the ratio of consumption to gross national product in order to release a rising fraction of resources for capital formation. The Turkish Five-Year Development Plan, 1963–67, projected a decline in the consumption ratio of nearly one percentage point per year, i.e. from 87·6 per cent in 1962 to 83·4 per cent in 1967.[1] Judged by the standard of accomplishments in other developing countries, this planned reduction in the consumption ratio was exceptionally rapid. Yet it was central to the Turkish strategy of development that a reallocation of this magnitude be accomplished. Similar strategies of reallocation undoubtedly will appear in future plans as well. It is timely, therefore, to examine the historical pattern of allocation and, in particular, to compare allocations to development with those made to military activities. The state has exercised a determinative influence over both and each has been crucial in bringing Turkey to the threshold of self-sustaining economic advance.

We shall investigate the allocation pattern in four ways. First, the pattern will be defined in terms suitable to the Turkish case, but terms which also have general applicability to other countries where the necessary data are available. Second, estimates of military expenditures and the other expenditure aggregates will be made and interpreted. Third, the historical allocation pattern will be evaluated from Turkish and foreign points of view to ascertain what differences, if any, emerge. Finally, certain cautions concerning the evaluation of military expenditures are expressed so that comparisons with development expenditures may be placed on a more nearly objective basis. We have no special case to make here in favour of or against any historical or future pattern of allocation, but we do advocate the collection and analysis of data which can help historians, economists, and policy-makers to reach their own judgments concerning this vital matter.

## THE ALLOCATION PATTERN: CONCEPTS

The volume of resources allocated annually to all domestic activities is customarily defined as the annual flow of gross national product plus imports minus exports. Both goods and services are included. The disposal of this flow is customarily traced to a set of final uses defined as private consumption, government consumption, private civilian capital formation and government civilian capital formation. Expenditures of resources on military services are customarily submerged within the larger category of government consumption. Here three changes will be made: (1) military expenditures will be separated and quantified in a category of their own; (2) expenditures on civilian capital formation will be combined with government expenditures on education and health to form a new classification designated development expenditure; and (3) the distinction between private and government institutions will be dropped. These changes will focus attention on the distribution of resources among three different types of activities—consumption, development and military—without regard to which types of institutions, private or public, absorb the resources.

Military expenditures will be defined as the value of resources absorbed into the military establishment, in this case the Turkish defence department, with one exception. Expenditures by other departments for primarily military purposes, such as for strategic highway and communications projects, will be included in so far as the North Atlantic Treaty Organization (NATO) definitions have permitted their inclusion. Thus, apart from this exception, the distinction between expenditures on military and non-military *activities* will correspond with a distinction between absorption by military and civilian *institutions*.

Military activities in Turkey encompass a wide range of public tasks. In general, the military establishment has maintained armed forces to deter or, upon occasion, to threaten adjacent countries. Specific objectives have included the stabilization of borders with six contiguous countries, the annexation of Hatay province, and the exertion of pressure on behalf of ethnic Turks residing in neighbouring territories. The Cyprus problem is an example of the last mentioned. The military have also controlled dissident groups internally, as for example during the Kurdish rebellion in the 1920s, and have supported or replaced civilian agencies in the maintenance of law and order during periods of restive political change, as in the late 1950s and following the military revolution of 27 May 1960.

Turkish forces have also participated in NATO and were active in the United Nations military operation in Korea. Thus, the concept of military activity gathers together a diverse set of tasks.

The value of military services will be measured statistically by the volume of resources entering the military activity. Thus, expenditures will be accepted as a measure of the value of military services. The activities defined as military frequently contribute simultaneously to the realization of additional objectives which bear the name of altogether different activities. The converse is also true of the development and consumption activities. The statistical treatment of expenditures which produce multiple kinds of benefits is illustrated by roads. Those which primarily, but not exclusively, carry military traffic will be charged as military expenditure, whereas other roads which primarily, but not exclusively, carry civilian traffic will be entered as development expenditure. The rule will be to assign expenditures to one or another of the three categories according to whichever expresses the principal intended use of the output. When an activity produces products serving more than one of the objectives, such as in the road illustration, some allocation rule has to be adopted and this one has the virtue of simplicity. Even though expenditures of one type may serve the objectives of another type in addition, these "spillover" consequences usually will be offsetting to some extent. Thus, the quantitative aggregates which will be produced by the rule will be an approximate, even if imperfect, description of the proportions in which resources have been applied to the pursuit of military objectives, development objectives, and consumption objectives respectively.

## The Size of Turkish Military Expenditure

Because the measurement of military expenditures presents some unfamiliar problems, it will be explained separately first. The flow of real resources into Turkish military activity has had two main streams which differ according to their systems of financing and procurement. One part has been acquired by the ordinary processes of Turkish government procurement, personnel employment, and conscription. The other part has been a flow of deliveries to the Turkish military organization from the United States government consisting of military equipment, supplies, and services. Over the years 1948–62 the ratio has been about two of conventional procurement to one of direct delivery from the U.S.

The budget of the Turkish ministry of defence (closed accounts) covers that part of the flow which is acquired by ordinary procurement processes. An alternative way of measuring the same flow is to use a time series for Turkish "defence expenditure" published by the North Atlantic Treaty Organization. It is based on reports by the Turkish government which endeavour to include all expenditures of a military nature whether made by the defence ministry or some other agency such as the highway department. The Turkish estimates are reviewed by the NATO secretariat and are probably very close to the definition of military expenditure used in this paper, except that they do not include direct U.S. deliveries which we shall add in separately.[2]

Direct American deliveries to the Turkish military organization have been financed by the multi-country U.S. military assistance programme (MAP). Unlike other international movements of goods and services financed by foreign aid, these transactions have not created a record in the Turkish import statistics. The statistical conventions of the United Nations system of national accounts, of the International Monetary Fund's *Balance of Payments Yearbook*, and of official agencies in the U.S. and Turkey, have all treated the MAP deliveries as government consumption in the U.S., not as real resources which were finally expended in Turkey as they, in fact, were. An additional effect of this statistical practice has been to omit the movement of such goods and services from the world's international trade statistics. Consequently, the trade data yield only a partial description of international commodity and service movements.

The IMF's *Balance of Payments Manual* proposes a theoretically consistent treatment as follows:[3]

> "When military end-items are granted by one country to another, the transfer is for the benefit of both countries. Since there has been a transfer of ownership to the goods, there is no doubt, however, that an economic transaction has taken place, and the theoretical treatment in this case does not present any problems, although it is difficult in practice to obtain information on such transactions. For pragmatic reasons, therefore, they are often treated for national accounts purposes as final government expenditure in the granting country, the international transfer being disregarded and excluded from the balance of payments. While such a treatment may prove necessary in practice, it is not recommended in this Manual, since it would be inconsistent with its basic principles. To make the reported data comparable between countries, it may be advisable to make some *ad hoc* exceptions to these principles in the requests for data, but such exceptions are

not made in the Manual itself, which is intended to provide a theoretical framework for the compilation of the balance of payments. In every respect, military end-items are treated in this Manual in the same way as other goods and services."

In the Turkish case, the MAP data have been published by the U.S. government, even though the IMF, itself, has consistently omitted them from its published accounts. Since the purpose of the present study is to take a comprehensive view of Turkey's economic transactions, the theoretically consistent practice of including the MAP data will be followed below.

Bringing the so-called "military" assistance flow within the system of international accounts and tracing it to final uses in the recipient country will place it on the same footing as the so-called "economic" assistance flow which has always been included. This is consistent with the fact that both flows transfer real resources from one nation to the other and that neither flow can properly be regarded, therefore, as consumption by the donor country. Further proof of this proposition is that Turkish policy-makers have regarded the expenditure of aid flows in Turkey as their activity and as a beneficial one to be defended against reduction. While it is true that policy-makers in the donor countries have also believed aid to be beneficial to them, that fact is not contradictory; it only calls attention to the joint interest which lies behind such resource transfers.

Aid has usually been classified according to the labels on the appropriations which financed it (e.g., in the U.S. there has been military assistance, defence support, supporting assistance, surplus commodity assistance, and others). The ultimate purposes served, or intended to be served, have departed widely from the financial classification at times. In the 1950s, economists recognized this difference between consequences and financial name-tags when they reasoned that "defence support" aid, which accompanied "military" aid, was really aiding Turkey's economic development, because Turkey appeared to be using the extra resources to expand both development and military expenditure. In the U.S. Congress, on the other hand, a theory was propounded that "defence support" financed deliveries to the civilian economy in Turkey in order to release equal amounts of local resources for the military establishment. Thus, it was understood that aid resources were transferable, but it was not clear whether transfers were serving developmental or military purposes and in what proportions.

In the estimates of military expenditure which follow immediately below, resources obtained by ordinary procurement processes and from the MAP are added together regardless of the purposes of aid. Because of the comments above, it should be understood that the MAP flow was not necessarily the only contribution of the U.S. to military expenditure in Turkey or necessarily even a solely military contribution, because transfers could have been made away from the military establishment as well. What probably happened in reality was that the availability of MAP tended to make ordinary military procurement smaller than otherwise, but the availability of other types of assistance encouraged an opposite tendency. These influences, or determinants, of final volumes of expenditures are irrelevant, however, to the measurement of actual expenditure which will be accomplished simply by adding up the quantities which were used in the military activity. This is done in Table 1.

The data on military expenditures are in current prices which rose approximately threefold over the period 1948–62. Being confined to one class of expenditure, they do not indicate very much about allocation. However, we shall compare the military expenditures with other aggregates, also in current prices, at a later stage. The advantage of using data in current prices for such comparisons is that they reflect the relative scarcities of the different kinds of resources

TABLE 1: MILITARY EXPENDITURES IN CURRENT PRICES, 1948–62
(Million TL)

| *Calendar years* | *Defence Ministry budget* (1) | *NATO Definition of defence expenditure* (2) | *Military assistance imports* (3) | *Total military expenditure* (2+3) (4) |
|---|---|---|---|---|
| 1948 | 377 | 530 | 203 | 733 |
| 1949 | 395 | 556 | 156 | 712 |
| 1950 | 442 | 599 | 131 | 730 |
| 1951 | 468 | 652 | 165 | 817 |
| 1952 | 611 | 725 | 409 | 1,134 |
| 1953 | 711 | 827 | 491 | 1,318 |
| 1954 | 834 | 936 | 620 | 1,556 |
| 1955 | 1,161 | 1,077 | 465 | 1,542 |
| 1956 | 979 | 1,159 | 482 | 1,641 |
| 1957 | 1,060 | 1,266 | 824 | 2,090 |
| 1958 | 1,396 | 1,470 | 2,264 | 3,734 |
| 1959 | 1,736 | 2,153 | 1,128 | 3,281 |
| 1960 | 1,728 | 2,410 | 786 | 3,196 |
| 1961 | 2,114 | 2,718 | 750 | 3,468 |
| 1962 | 2,556 | 2,970 | 1,419 | 4,389 |
| Ratios to total, 15-year average | 55% | 66% | 34% | 100% |

*Sources:*

Col. 1: Closed accounts except 1961–62 which are budget estimates. From 1950 onwards, years begin March 1. The fourteen-month budget starting 1 January 1949 has been adjusted to an annual basis to obtain the 1949 figure. For 1948–49, Türkiye Büyük Millet Meclisi, *Tutanak Dergisi*, VIII, 3, v. 16 (a), 1949, p. 274 ff., and 4, v. 24 (2), 1950, p. 148 ff. For 1950–62, *Plan*, Table 19.

Col. 2: For 1948, an estimate made on the assumption that the ratio of col. 2 to col. 1 was the same in 1948 as in 1949. For 1949–60, NATO, Information Service, *NATO: Facts about the North Atlantic Treaty Organization*, Paris, 1962, p. 105. For 1961–62, U.S. Department of Defense, *Military Assistance Facts*, Washington, 1963, p. 30. The NATO definition includes expenditures by other ministries primarily for military purposes, and was not subject to variations in accounting practices that disturb the data in col. 1.

Col. 3: Data are for deliveries. For Greece–Turkey aid, 1948–51, IMF, *Balance of Payments Yearbook*, Turkey sheets, October 1954, where the amount of military aid is identified. Verified by cross-check with amounts stated in Congressional hearings. For MAP, 1950–62, Department of Defense, *op. cit.*, pp. 30–1. A cross-check was made against data given on a U.S. fiscal year basis in Agency for International Development, *U.S. Foreign Assistance*, 1945–62, Washington, rev., 1963, p. 23. The AID series adds to a slightly larger total than does the Department of Defense series. Data in dollars were converted to lira at the principal end-of-year dollar rates for imports: For 1948–56, 2·82; for 1957, 3·96; for 1958–59, 9·02; for 1960–62, 9·04.

allocated to each type of expenditure as those scarcities have changed over the period.

There are several technical points to be made about the military data which, taken together, indicate that the estimates probably have a tendency to understate the absolute and relative levels of military expenditure.

1. For measurement purposes, it is desirable that the dollar values given to MAP import items indicate their market values, but many of the items had no meaningful markets. A case in point is that of advanced military equipment whose development cost usually is a high proportion of total cost. Since the MAP has been a small customer relative to other buyers, it was possible to charge the programme on a variety of bases ranging from incremental production cost to average full cost. Second-hand equipment which was about to become obsolete also could be priced at a bargain or charged at high prices to recoup funds from the MAP for other programmes.[4] When items were finally declared surplus, however, no charge could be made.[5] Lacking markets and consistent pricing practices, it is impossible to decide whether undervaluation, or even overvaluation, characterized the dollar pricing of MAP items.

2. We converted dollar values into Turkish lira values in order

to render the MAP imports comparable with other resource-flow measurements. The principal official import rate was used for this purpose. During the years 1953–57 this rate averaged perhaps half what an equilibrium rate would have been. Thus, for those years at least, the use of official rates undervalues the flow of MAP imports relative to the other resource flows. This downward bias also affects the measurement of consumption and development expenditures, but not to the same extent, since the import content was less in their cases and the investment estimates include corrections which place them on an "actual dollar cost" basis.

3. For measurement purposes, one wants relative prices which reflect equilibrium values, but the Turkish government has purchased many goods and services at prices which diverge from this criterion. For example, troops have been transported on the state railways at a loss to the carrier. Also, at one time in the mid-1950s cereals were "purchased" from the state trading organization by the army but not paid for. The divergence of Turkish prices from equilibrium values affects the measurement not only of military expenditures, but of consumption and development expenditures also. Perhaps price controls, which can be a major cause of undervaluation, were enforced more consistently for military buyers than for others, but one cannot be certain.

4. Conscription is a method of obtaining resources without paying their full transfer price, and Turkey has relied on conscription to raise most of its military force of half a million men.[6] How much more would have had to be paid, both in cash wages and provisioning in kind, to raise the same number of men on a voluntary basis is impossible to ascertain.[7] If a higher price would have had to be paid, that fact would mean that the data for military expenditure undervalue the real contribution which was made by manpower.[8]

5. The Turkish military forces use some facilities for which they have not paid, a particularly important case being the NATO infrastructure installations. Turkey has contributed a tiny part of the cost of the entire European infrastructure programme (e.g. it was 1·1 per cent in 1962), yet she has utilized pipeline, airfield, communication, and other facilities which NATO has built at NATO expense in Turkey.[9]

These qualifications, taken as a whole, indicate that the estimates of military expenditure probably understate the true values. Because the undervaluation of foreign exchange was quantitatively important, and this error was concentrated in the three years leading up to 1958, the greatest bias probably can be ascribed to that particular period. Apart from this, no trend can be ascribed to the bias on the basis of present information.

## THE ALLOCATION PATTERN: ESTIMATES AND THEIR INTERPRETATION

Combining the estimates of military expenditure with data for the other aggregates gives a comprehensive set of estimates for the sources and uses of resources which is presented in Table 2. It is

TABLE 2: TOTAL RESOURCES AND THEIR DISPOSAL IN CURRENT PRICES, 1948–62
(Billion TL)

| *Calendar years* | *Gross national product* | *Import surplus* | *Total resources* | *Expenditures* | | |
|---|---|---|---|---|---|---|
| | | | | *Military* | *Development* | *Consumption* |
| | (1) | (2) | (3) | (4) | (5) | (6) |
| 1948 | 10·1 | 0·4 | 10·5 | 0·7 | 1·4 | 8·4 |
| 1949 | 9·3 | 0·3 | 9·6 | 0·7 | 1·5 | 7·4 |
| 1950 | 10·4 | 0·2 | 10·6 | 0·7 | 1·6 | 8·3 |
| 1951 | 12·3 | 0·4 | 12·7 | 0·8 | 1·9 | 10·0 |
| 1952 | 14·3 | 0·9 | 15·2 | 1·1 | 2·5 | 11·6 |
| 1953 | 16·8 | 0·9 | 17·7 | 1·3 | 2·9 | 13·5 |
| 1954 | 17·1 | 1·1 | 18·2 | 1·6 | 3·3 | 13·3 |
| 1955 | 21·1 | 0·8 | 21·9 | 1·5 | 4·1 | 16·3 |
| 1956 | 24·3 | 0·5 | 24·9 | 1·6 | 4·6 | 18·7 |
| 1957 | 30·5 | 0·9 | 31·4 | 2·1 | 5·5 | 23·9 |
| 1958 | 38·5 | 2·6 | 41·1 | 3·7 | 6·8 | 30·5 |
| 1959 | 47·7 | 2·2 | 49·9 | 3·3 | 9·1 | 37·6 |
| 1960 | 51·0 | 1·8 | 52·8 | 3·2 | 10·1 | 40·0 |
| 1961 | 53·7 | 1·9 | 55·6 | 3·5 | 10·5 | 41·6 |
| 1962 | 60·7 | 3·5 | 64·3 | 4·4 | 11·8 | 48·1 |

Col. 1: For 1948–54, İstatistik Umum Müdürlügü, *Türkiye Milli Geliri, 1948–1957*, Ankara, 1958, No. 382, p. 4; for 1955–62, Devlet İstatistik Enstitüsü, *Türkiye Milli Geliri, 1948, 1955–1962*, Ankara, 1964, No. 456, p. 8. 1962 estimates are preliminary.

Col. 2: The import surplus is the excess of goods and services imports over goods and services exports. Imports financed by military assistance are included. For estimates of the import surplus on the basis of conventional definitions which exclude military, I used IMF, *Yearbook*, Turkey sheets of October 1954, December 1955, April 1961, April 1963, and July 1963. The 1962 estimates are preliminary. For estimates of imports financed by military assistance, see Table 1, col. 3. Data in dollars were converted to lira at end-of-year official rates the same as noted in Table 1, col. 3. For the years 1953–57, the use of official exchange rates seriously undervalues the import surplus.

Col. 3: = col. 1+col. 2 = col. 4+col. 5+col. 6.

Col. 4: Table 1, col. 4.

Col. 5: Kenan Gürtan's estimates of fixed capital formation were used as a starting-point. Estimates of annual increases in stocks and outlays on government health and education programmes were then added. Gürtan's estimates are based on the value of imports and local production of machinery, suitably raised to cover transportation and installation, plus estimates of construction based upon government construction expenditures, building permits, and other indirect evidence. Gürtan's import valuations are "actual dollar cost" inclusive of premiums paid to private parties to acquire licences or exchange and other unofficial charges. State sector imports were valued at official rates. *Türkiye'de Yatırımlar*, İktisat Fakültesi No. 110, Istanbul, 1959; State Planning Organization, *A Report Concerning the Correction and Standardization of Investment Accounts*, Ankara, 1962; and unpublished sheet of the State Institute of Statistics for data covering 1961 and 1962 prepared under Gürtan's direction. For increases in stocks plus health and education expenditure, I have added five per cent of GNP in each year. The health and education budgets totalled two per cent of GNP at the beginning of the period and three per cent at the end. Because the growth rate of real GNP declined over the period as a whole, I assume that the share of GNP going to accumulation of stocks also declined. In the absence of definite figures I assume three per cent for stocks at the beginning of the period, falling to two per cent at the end.

Col. 6: Estimated as a residual. Col. 6 = col. 3 − col. 4 − col. 5.

Computations were made in millions, but rounded to nearest tenths of billions for presentation.

convenient to re-express these estimates as ratios, either to GNP or to total resources, in order to make the pattern comparable over time independently of changes in the total volume of resources or the price level.[10] Ratios for this purpose are presented in Table 3 and it is these which will be used in the following discussion. A column showing the growth in real GNP has also been added in Table 3.

Because the estimates of the different aggregates vary in their degree of accuracy, this fact has to be taken into account when interpreting the data. The data for military expenditure are from a combination of Turkish and American public accounts which may be presumed accurate within the limits of the valuation problems already discussed. The estimates for development expenditure, as explained in the notes to the table, were taken from a special study of investment by Kenan Gürtan in which he followed a standard technique for countries lacking complete information and based his figures on imports of capital goods, local production, construction permits, government investment accounts, and other partial or indirect evidence. The least satisfactory estimates are those for consumption, because they are residuals which are affected by all the errors elsewhere in the accounts. In addition, annual variation in the rate of accumulation of inventories has not been removed from the residual and placed in the development expenditure account as would be desirable. This probably explains the fact that the ratio of consumption to GNP is correlated positively with annual changes in GNP when an opposite relationship is normally expected.

TABLE 3: TOTAL RESOURCES AND THEIR DISPOSAL EXPRESSED IN RATIOS, 1948–62
(Percentages to GNP)

| Calendar years | Gross national product (1) | Import surplus (2) | Total resources (3) | Expenditures: Military (4) | Expenditures: Development (5) | Expenditures: Consumption (6) | Index of real GNP 1948 = 100 (7) |
|---|---|---|---|---|---|---|---|
| 1948 | 100 | 4·3 | 104·3 | 7·3 | 13·8 | 83·2 | 100 |
| 1949 | 100 | 3·4 | 103·4 | 7·7 | 16·1 | 79·6 | 89 |
| 1950 | 100 | 2·3 | 102·3 | 7·0 | 15·2 | 80·0 | 103 |
| 1951 | 100 | 3·2 | 103·2 | 6·7 | 15·2 | 81·3 | 119 |
| 1952 | 100 | 6·4 | 106·4 | 7·9 | 17·6 | 80·9 | 129 |
| 1953 | 100 | 5·2 | 105·2 | 7·8 | 17·1 | 80·2 | 144 |
| 1954 | 100 | 6·2 | 106·2 | 9·1 | 19·5 | 77·7 | 131 |
| 1955 | 100 | 4·0 | 104·0 | 7·3 | 19·4 | 77·2 | 141 |
| 1956 | 100 | 2·3 | 102·3 | 6·7 | 18·8 | 76·7 | 150 |
| 1957 | 100 | 3·0 | 103·0 | 6·8 | 18·0 | 78·2 | 160 |
| 1958 | 100 | 6·8 | 106·8 | 9·7 | 17·7 | 79·3 | 179 |
| 1959 | 100 | 4·6 | 104·6 | 6·9 | 19·0 | 78·7 | 187 |
| 1960 | 100 | 3·6 | 103·6 | 6·3 | 19·7 | 77·6 | 191 |
| 1961 | 100 | 3·5 | 103·5 | 6·5 | 19·5 | 77·5 | 189 |
| 1962 | 100 | 5·8 | 105·8 | 7·2 | 19·5 | 79·1 | 201 |
| Average, 15 years | 100 | 4·4 | 104·4 | 7·3 | 18·6 | 78·6 | |
| | | | (Percentages to total resources) | | | | |
| Average, 15 years | 95·7 | 4·3 | 100 | 7·0 | 17·8 | 75·3 | |

*Source:* Calculated from Table 2. The estimates of real GNP are from the State Institute of Statistics. See source given in Table 2, col. 1.

With respect to the sources of resources, the IMF estimates of exports and imports (net imports) are used, although they are weak at the beginning of the period. The valuation biases on account of the exchange rate have already been mentioned. Two tests which lead to qualifications on the estimates of GNP will also be noted. First, the real growth rates for the separate subdivisions of national product were found to be as follows:

| *Sector* | *Per cent per annum* * |
|---|---|
| Agriculture (farming, forestry, and fishing) | 4·3 |
| Industry (manufacturing, mining, construction and utilities) | 6·5 |
| Services (trade, transport, government, dwellings, professions, and other services) | 7·3 |
| Net domestic product | 5·7 |

* Based on five-year averages centred on the terminal years of 1950 and 1960. Compound rates.

It is a rare country in which services grow appreciably more rapidly than both the total product and, even more significantly, than industry. Since no special factors appear to explain the Turkish performance, there is a question as to whether these data exaggerate the growth of national product.

The second test concerns agriculture and leads to a similar doubt. Because the crop area was extended rapidly in the late 1940s and early 1950s, and there also was an increase in the higher valued crops relative to others, it is conceivable that Turkish agriculture expanded with unusual vigour. To exceed three per cent over a long period is a major achievement, however, and questions about the data have arisen. The State Planning Organization criticized the accuracy of the increase recorded in 1958, basing its view primarily upon reports of agricultural experts who toured the crop areas that year. In addition, agricultural economists have thought that they found inconsistencies between recorded production increases, on one side, and records of crop marketings or of yields on state farms, on the other side. Consequently, there may have been some exaggeration, but the evidence is not so strong as to warrant definite conclusions, and some of the error may have referred only to annual variation and not to trend. If the more severe criticisms are accepted, the trend of agricultural production would have to be lowered from its recorded level of 4·3 per cent to a level of about three per cent.

In the face of inaccurate data for GNP, the most secure basis for considering the pattern of allocations is to study military and development expenditures alone, and to relate these two flows to each other rather than to GNP. When this is done, as in the bottom panel of Diagram 1, the fact emerges that resources not used for consumption have been allocated increasingly toward development and less toward military expenditure. The trend is irregular over time.

DIAGRAM 1: RATIO OF DEVELOPMENT AND MILITARY EXPENDITURES TO GNP

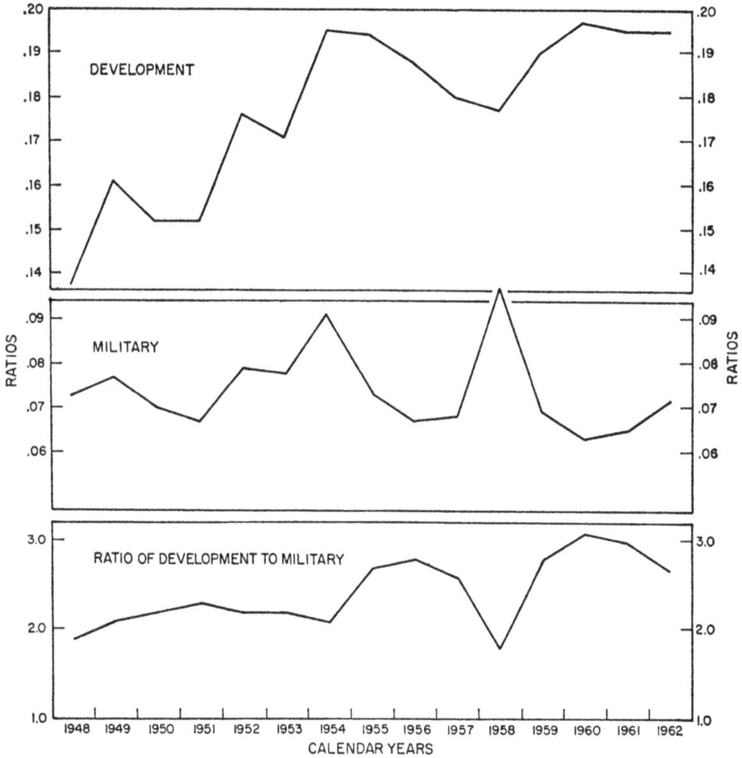


There are many reasons for focusing on the general shift of emphasis in the allocation of non-consumed resources rather than attaching significance to the year-to-year variations or the main change which appears to occur around the centre of the time period. Military deliveries were "lumpy" in the accounts, and the dating of investment flows presented problems in the Gürtan study. The effect of undervaluing foreign exchange impinged on both the military and development accounts, but presumably a little more on the former than the latter because of a higher import content. Consequently, in a period of significant undervaluation, such as the three years preceding 1958, the ratio of development to military may be somewhat overstated and the shift toward development may have occurred less at the centre of the time period and more towards the end. In any case, financial transactions provide a report on what happened at only one point in a long sequence of decisions and actions which had their beginnings at earlier dates and their final consequences much later. These qualifications do not detract, however, from the principal finding, which is that development expenditures have risen significantly relative to military expenditures during this fifteen-year interval. If the figures are accepted as they stand, there was an increase of forty-two per cent in the ratio of development to military between the beginning and the end of the period, measuring the terminal values by three-year averages.

Turkey's reduced emphasis on the military relative to economic development must be counted a remarkable achievement considering the massive infusion of American military aid at the time and the aggravated state of the cold war. This shift may not have been nearly as significant, however, as the fact that the growth of military expenditure over the period as a whole appears to have been at about the same speed as the growth of Turkey's own productive capacity as measured by GNP. This information, which comes from Diagram 1, is subject to the qualifications that annual variations have been so great as to make the discernment of general trends difficult, and furthermore, that the effects of inaccuracies in the recorded rate of growth for GNP need to be considered. Concerning the discernment of trend, the data suggest that within the period as a whole there apparently were two phases—military expenditures grew slightly faster than GNP in the first half of the period and slightly slower in the second. The second phase of slower growth in military expenditure offers a pattern which, if continued and reinforced in the future, would be the most favourable one from the standpoint of economic development.

Concerning the effect of errors in the recorded growth of GNP, if the rate were placed at five per cent instead of the recorded 5·7 per cent, both the military and development curves in Diagram 1 would be rotated slightly in the direction of a positive slope. Quantitatively, this would raise the 1962 values relative to the 1948 values by 0·5 and 1·3 percentage points respectively. In the case of military expenditures, this would not be a large enough change seriously to challenge the conclusions already reached, so this particular problem of inaccuracy needs no further consideration at this point. The conclusion stands that military expenditures grew about as fast as GNP over the years 1948–62 taken as a whole, but apparently grew faster in the early years and somewhat slower in the later ones.

## The Allocation Pattern From Turkish and Foreign Points of View

The Turkish government necessarily has a view of the allocation pattern, whether formulated explicitly or not, because its own policies shape that pattern. The chief obstacle in the way of taking an explicit view is the inherent difficulty of aggregating policies that have numerous special purposes as their objectives in addition to their affecting resource allocation. For example, credit policies affect, at one and the same time, both the delicate question of the division of credits between private and public enterprises and the magnitude of investment expenditure. A similar multiplicity of consequences characterizes taxes, public spending, controls over foreign exchange, institutional changes, and practically all the other economic activities of the government. It is only recently, with the advent of economic planning, that a systematic method has come into use for summarizing all the effects of policies on resource allocation and growth, and of striking a balance with each of the special objectives for which policies exist.

Foreign governments have necessarily had a view of the Turkish allocation pattern also, since, in a number of cases, they have been contributing resources to build up one or more of the final expenditure flows. They, too, have needed a means for co-ordinating their policies according to a consensual view of allocation objectives. By the mid-1960s co-ordination was being accomplished to a limited extent through intergovernmental consultations held by the Organization for European Co-operation and Development, but during most of the period considered here there was no unified view. Even within the American government, where most of the aid originated, interdepartmental fragmention of responsibility prevented a common view from emerging except under the most severe conditions of crisis. Because the interests of the aid-giving governments and the Turkish government necessarily come together at some point in the matter of aid, it is an appropriate subject on which to base a discussion of the differences in foreign and Turkish points of view.

The aid-giving governments have expended a great deal of effort in tying aid to specific projects and to transferring it in physical forms that would guarantee only those uses they preferred. Apart from incidental values, such as developing markets for certain products and creating opportunities for foreign technicians to participate, the tying of aid has actually had little effect of its own

TABLE 4: FORMS OF UNITED STATES ASSISTANCE TO TURKEY, 1948–62

| | *Million dollars* | *Per cent of total* |
|---|---|---|
| 1. Military items and services | 2,015 | 53 |
| 2. Surplus agricultural commodities | 418 | 11 |
| 3. Capital project items and services | 230 | 6 |
| 4. Technical co-operation services and supporting items | 38 | 1 |
| 5. Commodities not tied to projects or included elsewhere above | 1,113 | 29 |
| Total | 3,814 | 100 |

*Notes to the table*

Practically the whole of the fifteen-year import surplus of Turkey was made possible by U.S. assistance. The official record of U.S. assistance is classified according to the types of financing—e.g. military assistance grants, technical assistance grants, development loans, defence support grants, supporting assistance grants, sales for local currency, and so on. However, foreign aid eventually finances the movement of specific commodities and services, either because the aid was tied to the real items in the first instance or because it was expended for items selected subsequently. (Deferments of debt repayment are not counted here as aid.) In this table foreign aid is traced to the real items whose import into Turkey was financed. Their origin was the U.S. in a high percentage of cases, but also included third countries. The resulting table gives some idea of the kinds of items financed, although lack of information prevents us from achieving the standard international import classification. All data are for U.S. fiscal years.

*Military items and services.* The military assistance programme supplies aircraft, vehicles, tanks, weapons, missiles, ammunition, consumable items, and services such as shipping and training. Data are for net deliveries.

*Surplus agricultural commodities.* Sales to Turkey for lira under Title I of Public Law 480 have totalled $383 million and were divided among commodities and services as follows: wheat, 212; other cereals, 23; fats and oils, 98; miscellaneous commodities, 8; and shipping services, 41. These are the amounts which were authorized for sale. Deliveries were somewhat less, because of amounts in the "pipeline" at the end of the period and instances of under-utilization of sales authority. The other $35 million of surplus commodities was shipped as emergency or voluntary agency relief.

*Capital project items and services.* This category covers the imported components of the Ereğli iron and steel works (130) and such other projects as the improvement of the Zonguldak coal mines, the expansion of the Karabük steel mill, the erection of power plants and electric networks, and smaller private sector projects financed by the Industrial Development Bank. The services of foreign contractors during construction and running-in are included. The data cover Export-Import Bank projects and project loans by both AID and its predecessor agencies. Part of the amount was in the "pipeline" and hence undelivered at the end of the period.

*Technical co-operation services and supporting items.* This category covers the cost of AID technicians or sub-contractor personnel on technical assistance projects in agriculture, industry, transportation, labour, health, education, and public administration. Supporting equipment and supplies were also imported under this financing category.

*Commodities not tied to projects or covered elsewhere above.* This category consists mainly of commodity assistance. It includes such items as chemicals, wool, metals, pharmaceuticals, steel, paper, machinery, vehicles, tyres, and fertilizers. Included are imports financed by grants, commodity assistance loans, and funds supplied by the U.S. through the Organization for European Economic Co-operation and the European Payments Union. Those that were tied to projects and programmes under the other headings (lines 1 to 4) are shown there. A small amount of project assistance is merged with the commodity assistance estimates (line 5) only because it could not be segregated statistically (e.g. loans totalling $45 million in FY 1955 and FY 1956 were for a mixed package of commodity and project assistance). Of course, many commodities have gone to projects even when imported under the untied commodity assistance system. The administrative costs of the AID mission in Turkey are also covered by these figures, but the amounts are small relative to the total. Data are on an obligation or loan authorization basis.

*Reverse exports to the United States.* The data are gross in the sense that no deduction is made for commodities and services furnished to the U.S. government by Turkey in exchange for assistance. A rough estimate of such reverse exports is $80 million, which was financed by the counterpart funds arising from grant aid plus another $100 million which was financed by PL 480 sales for Turkish lira. Offsets for repayments in foreign exchange of loans do not have to be considered, since they are negligible to date. A second element of "grossness" is that the categories 2–5 are commitments of funds, a small part of which never actually resulted in shipments, particularly in the case of line 2.

*Sources.* AID, Statistics and Reports Division, *U.S. Foreign Assistance, 1945–62*, Washington, 1963, pp. iv–v, 23; AID, Office of the Controller, *Status of Loan Agreements*, Washington, 1964, pp. 66–7; AID, *Turkish Economic Statistics*, Ankara, 1963, pp. 42, 44, 45.

on the ultimate allocation of resources. This is because the transferability of resources in Turkey has always made it possible for government policy to turn specific resources into general resources by substituting aid resources for other resources at the margin. When the purposes of aid have been achieved, therefore, it has generally been because substantial agreement existed between the governments rather than because the aid-giving countries successfully compelled a reluctant Turkey to devote aid to specific uses by tying their aid to projects and specific forms.

Indeed, substitution processes have been recognized on both sides and exploited at times to make given amounts of aid accomplish more of the intended purposes than could be purchased some other way. For example, it was cheaper to supply commodities to Turkey which released productive workers for service in an expanded army than to supply foreign manpower directly to the army. Another example has been surplus food aid. Because of American farm policies, surplus foods have had a relatively low opportunity cost in aid programmes—countries usually could exchange given amounts of general commodity aid for larger amounts of food aid. Turkey has absorbed food aid partly by an increase in consumption, but also in part by releasing resources to serve developmental and military purposes instead of consumption.

In principle, the *form* of aid should be chosen on the basis of the comparative costs of local and foreign goods and services, whereas the *level* of aid should be related to an agreed target for the ultimate allocation of those extra resources which aid provides. The generous level of aid which Turkey has attracted from the U.S. and other nations presumably reflects foreign support for Turkey's allocational policies. However, when we make such a positive statement, we assume that assistance would not have continued to flow if the consensus among policy-makers in the aid-giving countries had disagreed significantly from the allocational objectives of Turkish policy-makers. If this were not so, we would have to conclude that donors have been prepared to pay a high and repetitive cost in resources which were, from their point of view, misallocated.

From the standpoint of development alone—leaving aside other uses of resources for the moment—the governments on both sides of an aid relationship usually can agree that the development ratio should be raised to the limits of absorptive capacity. This is in everyone's interest because it raises the economy's growth rate. An additional advantage from the standpoint of the aid-giving countries is that a higher growth rate in conjunction with a marginal saving ratio that exceeds the development ratio assures that the transition from dependence upon foreign aid to self-support will be shortened. In Turkey's case, the development ratio was moderately high by 1962, but not at a maximum. The First Five-Year Development Plan (1962–67) envisaged a further increase in the ratio of capital formation to GNP of three percentage points. To be effective in achieving the transition to self-support, however, high development ratios have to be accompanied by even higher marginal domestic savings ratios. Turkey's past performance with respect to savings is therefore of interest. It ought to be revealed by the allocation data. An unambiguous set of savings estimates is not forthcoming, however, because the results depend upon what assumptions are made concerning the purposes of aid. An example will illustrate the problem.

If we assume that the purpose of the foreign aid given to Turkey was to enlarge development expenditure, then gross domestic savings would be approximately equal to the difference between development expenditure and net imports, taking net imports to be approximately the value of foreign aid. In Diagram 2, the bottom curve was calculated on this assumption. The computation assumes, in effect, that all aid delivered in unsuitable forms for immediate expenditure on development (e.g. military goods, general import commodities, and food) was intended to be transformed into development resources by substitution processes. The assumption is extreme, and

DIAGRAM 2: RATIOS OF GROSS DOMESTIC SAVINGS TO GNP ASSUMING ALTERNATIVE PURPOSES OF AID

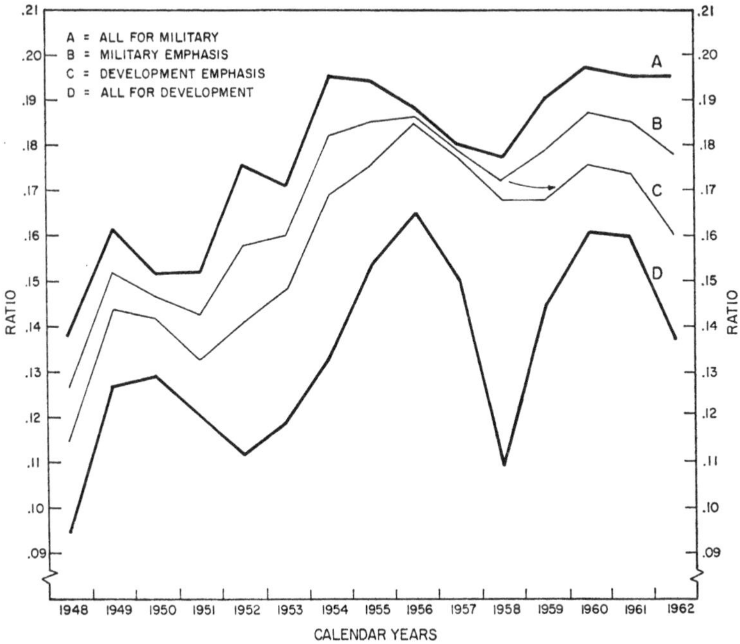


in the Turkish case goes too far. However, this is the assumption that is made in open-economy growth models and in national accounts statistics which measure domestic savings as the difference between investment outlays and net imports.

At the opposite extreme, it could be assumed that all aid was for military purposes, again irrespective of the initial forms of aid delivery. In this case, it would be assumed that development expenditure could only draw upon domestic saving for support. The domestic saving ratio would then be equal to the development ratio as shown by the top curve in Diagram 2. This has sometimes been the Soviet view of American aid to Turkey. According to this view, the sole purpose of the aid was to build up the Turkish military establishment. If that were the case, any resources diverted to development would be counted as saved by the domestic Turkish economy irrespective of their origin. If aid were given wholly for consumption, instead of for military use, the measurement of domestic saving would again be the same. Thus, the top curve in the diagram is an upper limit for the savings estimate.

All the realistic possibilities lie between the top and bottom curves. The quantity which domestic saving should measure is the contribution of the domestic economy to development (or to capital formation if a narrower definition were adopted). Unfortunately, the boundaries on this quantity are so far apart that they yield estimates of the level within only about five percentage points of a true value (leaving aside statistical error). The only safe conclusion regarding trend is that an increase of unspecified amount apparently took place over the period as a whole—we compare the highest early points with the lowest later points in order to disprove the existence of any slope other than a positive one. In order to make better estimates, information about the actual purposes of aid is required to decide what portion of development expenditure was covered by aid rather than by domestic savings. Two hypothetical estimates of domestic savings are presented below to illustrate the possibilities. Others could be constructed. These two assume that the purposes of foreign aid in Turkey were as follows respectively:

Curve B: *Resource transfers favoured the military and consumption was given a little.* In this case, it is assumed that the purposes of aid were to give the military an amount equal to MAP plus forty per cent of all other net imports, and to give consumption another ten per cent. In other words, the net effect, after all transfers, was that half of the non-MAP aid was given to support economic development.

Curve C: *MAP was for the military and the rest was for development.* In this case, the assumption of indirect support to the military is dropped. All aid, except MAP, is considered to have been for development, even including food shipments. Substitution processes were to be mobilized for the development task rather than for the promotion of military expenditure.

These two hypothetical calculations yield sharply different judgments about Turkey's own contribution to development during the period. If the purposes of aid had a development emphasis, as in curve C, then Turkey's contribution was smaller and that contribution deteriorated in the second half of the period. On the other hand, if the purposes of aid were more strongly non-developmental—i.e. oriented more towards military or consumption uses, as in curve B, then Turkey made a greater contribution to her own development, and sustained that contribution reasonably well in the last years of the period. The differences arise *only* because different norms as to the purposes of aid have been brought to bear in judging the historical events. The amounts of resources, after co-mingling domestic and foreign resources, are estimated no differently in the two cases.[11]

Since the purposes of aid also may change from time to time, the effect of such changes needs to be investigated. In 1958 Turkey experienced a severe international liquidity crisis, her internal debt was refinanced by a group of foreign governments and the IMF, and new commitments to stabilize the economy and promote development were made. The proportion of net imports provided by MAP declined sharply as the non-MAP forms of aid built up again. Curves B and C both reflect a decline in military emphasis to the extent that the MAP diminished in importance. However, they differ in their assumptions about the purposes of the non-MAP assistance. If the purposes of the latter also shifted from a partially military to an exclusively development purpose after 1958, the time path of that shift should be traced out. The relevant measure of domestic savings would move from curve B to C along some such path as the arrow which connects the two curves in the diagram. Even though hypothetical, this example shows what may have happened, or could happen, whenever the purposes of aid change. In effect, the recipient country must reallocate resources in accordance with the change in purposes, or the deviation will be calculated as due to its own saving behaviour.

Historical judgment concerning the domestic saving ratio is basically limited by two factors. One is the difficulty of observing the purposes of aid when a veil of financial captions and political interpretation is drawn across the transactions. The other is the simple possibility that the purposes of the parties to aid transactions may genuinely diverge. In the latter case, whose norms should be used? Since no general answer is possible, the economist and the historian have a responsibility to make their assumptions explicit and, whenever possible, to offer alternative interpretations.

From the standpoint of practical policy, this study of the Turkish case leads to a further general conclusion. Aid-givers and aid-receivers can only evaluate the saving performance of the recipient economy if they first agree upon the quantitative norms which will be used. Their choice is not a matter which can be left to economists, since it depends upon the very purposes of assistance and that is a matter for the responsible policy-makers.

## Comparing Military and Development Expenditures

Desirable as they might be, no general criteria are available to tell us how much a nation should spend of its resources on military activities or on development. Consequently, a historical judgment on the pattern of Turkish allocation is beyond our capability. By bringing data on Turkish military expenditure to the fore, however, and comparing them with estimates of development expenditure, we have made the economist's point of view evident. From his standpoint, allocation always involves alternatives. In the study of Turkish history this has sometimes been appreciated, sometimes not, and it would appear worth while to clarify some of the issues which have been raised.

In a nation struggling for its very existence, it is usual to think of military needs as having a first, and absolute, claim upon resources. During the Turkish War of Independence, 1919–22, sovereignty itself was the prize at stake, and from the nationalist movement's point of view, this one end was paramount. The idea of giving priority to one thing at a time, rather than balancing a number at once, is well expressed in the following description of Atatürk's strategy of modernization.[12]

". . . Where the Young Turks had tried to tackle the problems of security, identity, and modernization helter-skelter all at once, Kemal clearly sensed the need for priorities. Major issues were tackled one at a time: military defence (1919–22), the institutions of a new state (1923–24), and legal and cultural reforms (1924–28). Economics was added only to the end of this list. After the *étatist* decade of the 1930s, the mobilization of manpower in World War II (without corresponding industrial effort), and the decision in 1945–50 to move from authoritarian to democratic politics further delayed concerted attention to agricultural and industrial development. While 1908 in Turkey may be considered the analogue in political modernization to 1868 in Japan, the greater complexity of the political issues resulted in a further time-shift whereby the analogue of Japan's decades of economic development from 1870 to 1890 comes in Turkey, at best, in the 1950s and 1960s."

In this quotation, a priority concept was used to arrange things in a time sequence as if only one thing could be done at a time.

Governments are rarely limited, however, to such radical choices. Even Atatürk, as he sought support for his new policies and introduced them one at a time, was applying the power of the state and the economic resources of the nation at the same time to economic development. For example, the Ottoman debts were re-negotiated, railroads were nationalized and extended, a Turkish bank was formed, and a national strategy of development, however inelegant it might appear today, evolved. Thus, portions of the early Kemalist strategy of modernization went well beyond defence, the creation of governing institutions, and legal and cultural reforms, and had, instead, a major role in laying the foundations for economic development. The fact that everything goes on at once, with the modern state participating concurrently at many points, poses for political leaders the problem of fixing proportions rather than sequences. One view of their historical choices is given by the resource allocation pattern because it expresses a balance of action rather than a sequence.

Thus, the political historian has a resource allocation problem to explain just as surely as does the economist. The resource over which Atatürk disposed was a capacity to persuade and to compel. This resource was deployed over many fields simultaneously, so he had a continuous problem of deciding upon proportions. To have leapt from one exclusive application of political resources to another would have been fatal. Or to have ignored the scarcity of political resources relative to the useful things that political action might have accomplished would have led to the Young Turk phenomenon of over-commitment. A major factor in Atatürk's success was that he was a better optimizer, in the economist's sense, than his forerunners.

In Turkey more recently, a comparable problem of balancing has existed. The military organization has performed diverse services of varying essentiality, e.g. maintaining a large standing army, guarding the Ankara and Istanbul radio stations, manoeuvring along the Turkish–Syrian border when Syrian political events appeared to threaten Turkey, and making jet passes over Cyprus. However, it is not possible to say that a fixed amount of military expenditure—no less and no more—was necessary, because some valuable tasks should always be left untouched when resources are scarce. Ideally, the quantity of military services which Turkey purchased should have depended upon how far down a list of military services the government could go and still be getting increments which were worth their cost in terms of civilian alternatives foregone. Sovereignty, power, and security are all variable quantities, and they also may be increased at the margin by civilian as well as military means. Hence there are also questions of which means should be chosen, taking into account the comparative costs of alternative means which are foregone. This reasoning applies not only to military decisions, but also to the determination of development and consumption expenditure. Consequently, no judgment on the historical allocations to one use is legitimate if formed without regard to the alternative potentialities that existed at the time. Making use of this principle, we may say that the failure of the military ratio to decline more sharply in the last years of the period was probably due as much to lack of sufficient administrative and entrepreneurial vigour in the development of the economy as it was to a Turkish–American military security policy. The remedy, if a further shift from military to developmental objectives is wanted, lies in part, therefore, in creating more attractive development alternatives.

Recent writing on Turkey has stressed the role of the military as developers and shown that the military have made an extraordinary range of contributions.[13] In some cases, however, this writing is characterized by a habit of thought which stresses only the benefits of those things which have happened, without discussing other benefits which have been foregone in order to achieve the former results. The perils of speculating on what might have happened *if*... are well known. Yet it is valuable to speculate, because the habit of critical review may uncover alternatives which merit more general adoption in the future. Turkey has entered a phase of national development when it is important to know not only the story of the military as developers, but also the story of the developers themselves whatever their backgrounds.

The military establishment has been responsible for creating a great many values in addition to providing a primary output of military services. It has supplied *a reserve capacity for governing the nation*, which scholars have universally agreed was put to valuable use in 1960. It has furnished *a style of life* which the officer élite can enjoy for its own sake. It has given *training and experience* in the use of mechanical, technical, and communication skills to men who have subsequently rejoined the civilian labour force. It has built, or helped to build, *public works* such as highways, ports, and airfields, which are valuable for civilian activities too. It has been *a vehicle for importing and adapting Western* ideas in a country which has benefited greatly from the process of cultural borrowing. This is an impressive list; the military establishment has certainly contributed substantially to the making of a modern Turkish nation.

It has been but a step from these discoveries to the conclusion that there is something right, or at least fortunate, about the continuing growth of the military in developing countries. However, that step carries the enthusiasm of scholarly discovery too far, because it must also be asked whether there are alternative ways of securing these (secondary) benefits. Just as the (secondary) roles of the military deserve investigation, the (secondary) roles of development also need to be investigated and compared with the former.

If the objective is *to create reserve capacities for government*, they are also built by the experience and learning of men who solve rural development problems, manage large complexes of industry, organize labour, and administer departments of government. If the objective is *to create a style of life* which Turks value, that too is attainable by increasing people's participation in the income-producing jobs of development. If the objective is *to improve the quality of manpower*, working at the organizational, mechanical, and technical tasks that development programmes demand is a means to that end. If the objective is *to build public works*, one of the consequences of development is that the economic base available to finance and execute such works is enlarged. If the objective is *to capture the best ideas of the West* and to adapt them to Turkey's needs, one of today's international vehicles is the cultural and technological transfer which accompanies development programmes. Thus, the activity of development makes a powerful contribution to the same values which the Turkish military establishment has helped to create during its own special history.

Turkey has now come to a stage when civilian development and military activity are both capable of performing the ubiquitous tasks of modernization. In these circumstances, judgments concerning resource allocation should take into consideration the entire range of consequences on both sides of a comparison. As a matter of practical policy equal-cost projects at the margin of the military and development budgets should both be seen as producers of (secondary) benefits and these should be taken into consideration on the same terms.

The military are often given a substantial share of the credit for the Turkish highway development programme which achieved great success in the 1950s. However, study of the data reveals that only about one per cent of the expenditure on highway development from 1948 to 1960 was in some way made by the military establishment.[14] The military connection was that the Turkish and U.S. governments were persuaded to allocate resources to highway development to meet a need for greater mobility of military forces and supplies. Economic resources were absorbed and the task of road construction was performed largely by the civilian highway administration. It would be a strange kind of logic which credited the beneficiaries of a free service with having produced it, which is the way the highway case seems to have been interpreted. This is a case of developers providing something which has made the military more effective.

Another case of possible misinterpretation is manpower training by the military. Conscription brings many men into military service who are illiterate and otherwise poorly equipped to learn, communicate, and carry out technical tasks. The army has met this situation by establishing special literacy and technical schools. In this way, army training has improved the skills of the nation, but the extent and appropriateness of military training for subsequent civilian employment is easily exaggerated. The following data, collected in a national rural development survey in 1962, indicate that the role of military institutions in literacy training has been rather small, and declining, relative to the importance of other training institutions such as primary schools. Only about three per cent of the rural males who became literate during the decade ending in 1962 learned their skill in the army.

TABLE 5: THE MILITARY CONTRIBUTION TO MALE LITERACY

| | *Age Group* | | | |
|---|---|---|---|---|
| | *16–19* | *20–29* | *30–49* | *50+* |
| Percentage of male literates in age group who learned to read and write in military service | —* | 3 | 10 | 15 |
| Male literacy rate for the age group, percentage | 79 | 75 | 55 | 23 |

* Since conscripts usually serve at ages 18 and 19, no effect of military training appears in this age group.

*Source:* Frederick W. Frey kindly made this data available. Also see his "Surveying Peasant Attitudes in Turkey", *The Public Opinion Quarterly*, 27 (3), 1963, 335–55.

It is also useful to distinguish between *military men* and the *military organization*. Men with military backgrounds are prominent in Turkey's public life. Nevertheless, it has been exactly such men, e.g. Kemal Atatürk, İsmet İnönü, and Cemal Gürsel, who have helped develop stronger civilian processes of government and insisted that the military organization be confined to creditable performance in its own distinctive field. When a group of officers within the

Committee on National Unity entertained ideas of prolonging officer rule in 1961, they were reminded of the consensus in favour of civilian government and were then purged by their comrades. When men of any background assume high office, they become, by virtue of their offices, developers, because development is a pervasive activity of government today. The important questions are whether to undertake development tasks through defence ministries, public works administrations, or agricultural extension services, and these questions are best decided on the basis of project productivity and the ability to carry and enlarge institutional responsibilities.

Spokesmen for the U.S. Department of Defence have appeared to deny this distinction between military men and military organizations. Speaking of the Middle East generally, but referring frequently to Turkey as a case in point, a Deputy Assistant Secretary has said,[15] ". . . The U.S. accepts military control as a fact of life in many developing countries, and seeks [therefore ?] to promote a programme which aims toward maximum stability and nation-building activity in the military."

The bracketed word, *therefore*, is added to ask whether military control is a relevant consideration in deciding where to place development resources. The idea that military establishments should inaugurate "civic action programmes" and enter the business of economic development collides with an opposite and strong tradition of civil-military separation in Turkey. The Turkish army co-operates in local affairs wherever it is stationed and responds to civilian emergency situations. However, the Turkish leadership has consistently resisted attempts to blur what is regarded as an efficient specialization of function in the performance of public tasks.

The idea that *men* with distinguished military backgrounds can contribute leadership is also part of the Turkish tradition, but that fact is not a good guide to the allocation of resources among institutions. The career tracks by which the educated élite move upward in Turkey, and from which political leadership is recruited, have broadened significantly in the course of modernization. It would appear reasonable, therefore, to distribute investments in future leadership among a number of institutional vehicles rather than to concentrate them on the military alone. Turkey is a nation well advanced in her economic development which offers an expanding range of opportunities to her developers.

## NOTES

1. The ratio of consumption (both public and private) to GNP has been calculated from data appearing in State Planning Organization, *First Five-Year Development Plan, 1963–1967*, Ankara, 1963, p. 116, Table 49. This concept of consumption is not directly comparable with the one defined below for use in this study.

2. Published information concerning the NATO definition of military expenditure does not state explicitly that the flow of direct American deliveries has been excluded, but such an inference is supported by the following evidence: (1) The NATO figures are smaller than the sum of the defence ministry budget plus direct American deliveries (in Table 1, col. 1+col. 3>col. 2). (2) In the NATO statistics, the cost of the American military assistance programme is shown in the United States expenses. Consequently, the NATO data could only have avoided double counting by excluding those same amounts from the Turkish expenditure series. *Vide* Lord Ismay, Secretary General, *NATO—The First Five Years, 1949–1954*, Paris, n.d., p. 111, and the NATO source cited in support of Table 1, col. 2. The NATO purpose has been to find out how much defence activity each country finances itself, whereas our purpose is to measure the volume of real resources that are being used for military purposes by Turkey irrespective of financing. (3) Direct deliveries of American military goods and services have not usually been passed through the Turkish financial accounts. The Turkish budget law has included a passage every year that permitted the government to do so by adding military assistance deliveries to both the expenditure and revenue sides of the budget, but the authority has been used infrequently. In 1955 there was an irregular jump in the defence ministry budget (Table 1, col. 1). I am indebted to Oktay Yenal who discovered, in the course of his flow of funds analysis for Turkey, that this jump was due to the inclusion of a block of military aid for that single year. Small amounts were also added to the budgets in the years 1950–1952.

3. *Manual*, 3rd ed., Washington, 1961, para. 93.

4. E.g. Senate Committee on Appropriations, *Hearings on Economic Co-operation Administration*, H. R. 6801, Washington, 1948, p. 390.

5. Agency for International Development, Statistics and Reports Division, *U.S. Foreign Assistance, 1945–1962*, Washington, rev., 1963, p. v.

6. The size of the forces is assumed to be approximately equal to the number of males who were aged 18 and 19 in Turkey. The conscription law required two years of service commencing at age 18, or soon thereafter, and was strictly enforced. Few men were exempted. In addition, there was a core of volunteer warrant and senior officers.

7. Privates were paid a token cash wage, equivalent to ten U.S. cents per month. Officers were paid on civil service scales, but were kept one step higher than civilians with the same period of service and were paid supplementary allowances. University graduates were eligible for officer status during their military service.

8. Many conscripts received compensation, counting both cash compensation and material provisioning, during their conscript service which was greater than they could earn alternatively in civilian employment. However, they could not reallocate the income in kind they received to other purposes—for example, to their dependants. Such constraints on the manner in which income recipients could use their income were equivalent to negative income effects which need to be deducted from gross income to ascertain net remunerations. Thus we have

the following paradox: The physical well-being of many Turkish conscripts improved during military service, but their alternative civilian income—in cash, in kind, and in psychic form—would usually have been judged by the conscripts to be higher than the income they receive during military service. Certainly this would not be true of all the men who were conscripted, since some would have joined the forces voluntarily on the existing terms, but so long as the entire 500,000 men would not have volunteered, an element of undervaluation is present in the military expenditure account. It is in the nature of conscript labour that its value is understated by financial accounts.

9. Turkey's share in past expenditure is given in NATO, *op. cit.*, pp. 122–3. Details of the NATO expenditures in Turkey and the Turkish use of NATO facilities are not available.

10. This is not to say that the *processes* of growth or inflation do not exert an influence on the allocation ratios. Certainly they do. What we get from Tables 2 and 3 is an *ex post* description of the allocation of resources after all influences have made their mark.

11. The effect of reducing the measured growth rate for GNP would be to tilt the curves upward correspondingly. Since this would increase all their slopes, the conclusions reached here would have to be modified accordingly. See the earlier text for an experiment which illustrates the adjustment.

12. R. E. Ward and D. A. Rustow, *The Political Modernization of Turkey and Japan*, Princeton University Press, Princeton, 1964, p. 458.

13. The following examples, which are not an exhaustive list, may be cited: Daniel Lerner and Richard D. Robinson, "Swords into Plowshares: The Turkish Army as a Modernizing Force", *World Politics* 13 (1), October 1960, pp. 19–44: Sidney N. Fisher, "The Role of the Military in Society and Government in Turkey", in S. N. Fisher (ed.), *The Military in the Middle East*, Ohio State University Press, Columbus, 1963, pp. 21–40; Walter F. Weiker, *The Turkish Revolution 1960–61: Some Aspects of Military Politics*, Brookings, Washington, 1963; Dankwart A. Rustow, "Political Modernization and the Turkish Military Tradition" in Rustow and Ward, *op. cit.*, pp. 352–88; and Frederick W. Frey, "The Army in Turkish Politics", *Land Reborn* 11 (2), August 1960, pp. 3–14.

14. $5 million was allocated out of Greece–Turkey military aid and another $2·2 million was paid out of aid for Baghdad Pact roads. These figures and total highway costs are from Columbia University School of Law, *Public International Development Financing in Turkey*, New York, 1962, pp. 125, 128. We have not taken account of road maintenance (which is not development anyway), nor of other direct, in-kind contributions that the military may have made, but the amounts are believed to have been small. Cf. Robert Lehman, "Building Roads and a Highway Administration in Turkey", in Howard M. Teaf, Jr. and Peter G. Franck, *Hands Across Frontiers*, Cornell University Press, Ithaca, 1955, pp. 363–409.

15. Frank Keenan Sloan, "The Role of the Military in Development", in William R. Polk (ed.), *Developmental Revolution: North Africa, Middle East, South Asia*, Middle East Institute, Washington, 1963, p. 118.

CHAPTER 4

# Types of Rural Development

*by John F. Kolars*

IN rural Turkey the focus of life is the agricultural village. It is here that more than two-thirds of the Turkish population live and produce an agricultural output accounting for two-fifths of the national product of Turkey. Through a study of these agricultural communities, one can expect to unravel some of the dynamics of rural development in Turkey.

The villager has become important, because the regional and national development of Turkey must ultimately find some expression in the actions of the small rural community. These communities are neither static nor negligible in their influence on national affairs. They must be seen as constantly changing and as critical parts of the larger, integral social and economic milieu. No village exists today in Turkey which does not share to greater or less degree in the fortunes of the entire country. Touch one village, or touch one city, and reverberations will be felt over a wide area, in some cases over the entire system.

Studies of villagers and their villages have ranged from individual case studies to national surveys, and have encompassed such diverse topics as social attitudes and the cultivation cycles of specific crops.[1] The results reveal such variety along almost every important dimension that the terms "Turkish village" or, even more restrictively, "Anatolian village" are now hardly more than generic conveniences. The large-scale surveys are most useful in extending the geographic coverage, but are limited to a relatively few, easily observed, characteristics.[2] The case studies are more helpful in extending the historical perspective, breadth of detail, and insights. One of the challenges at this time is to compare the results of these separate studies in order to see what may be learned about the process of rural development in Turkey.

## REGULARITIES IN RURAL CHANGE

The transformation of traditional into modern societies has been studied by geographers and anthropologists throughout the world as a process of acculturation between the two predominant cultural types. In his summary of work in this field, George M. Foster identifies "cross-cultural regularities" in the processes of change which, he says, constitute "a level of theory with practical implications for developmental work".[3] Two of these regularities are especially useful in the analysis of the Turkish case. The first is that cities are focal points of change. Foster extends this idea to suggest that "a hard look at the nature and implications of village-urban relationships probably would inject more life into [rural] community development programmes than would any other single act".[4] The second is that "major shifts in the economic basis of livelihood" are central accompaniments to the acculturation process.[5] Among rural communities, the movement from subsistence to cash crops[6] is the principal form of this change. In Turkey, major shifts to cash crops are revealed by national crop data.[7] The present author has linked the rapidity of development along the southern Mediterranean coast to the introduction of cash crops into the villages he has studied there.[8]

Two interdependent themes are thus selected for this study of village Turkey: the changing relationship of the village to the urban centre, and the relationship between subsistence agriculture and the development of market-oriented activities which yield cash incomes. Later in this chapter, a typology will be presented which distinguishes among villages in terms of these two regularities of rural change.

## Prior Studies and Sources

In a comparative study of five Turkish villages displaying increasing degrees of isolation from modern urban centres, Muzaffer Sherif has found related differences in personality, potential for change, and technological development. Some of his important conclusions are:[9]

> The individual's mobility increases in proportion to contact with modern technology and is further enhanced by the pressures of local conditions (e.g. economic scarcity) away from the community. In the two villages summarized (Karlık and Beşikdüzü), local conditions forced villagers to leave both places to seek work; however, those who left Karlık [most isolated place] usually returned shortly, while many who left Beşikdüzü [least isolated place] were away for long periods or did not return. Ten families had left Beşikdüzü during the decade prior to the study and had not returned. In other words, the greater the degree of contact with modern means of transportation and other technological

# INDEX MAP OF TURKISH SETTLEMENTS

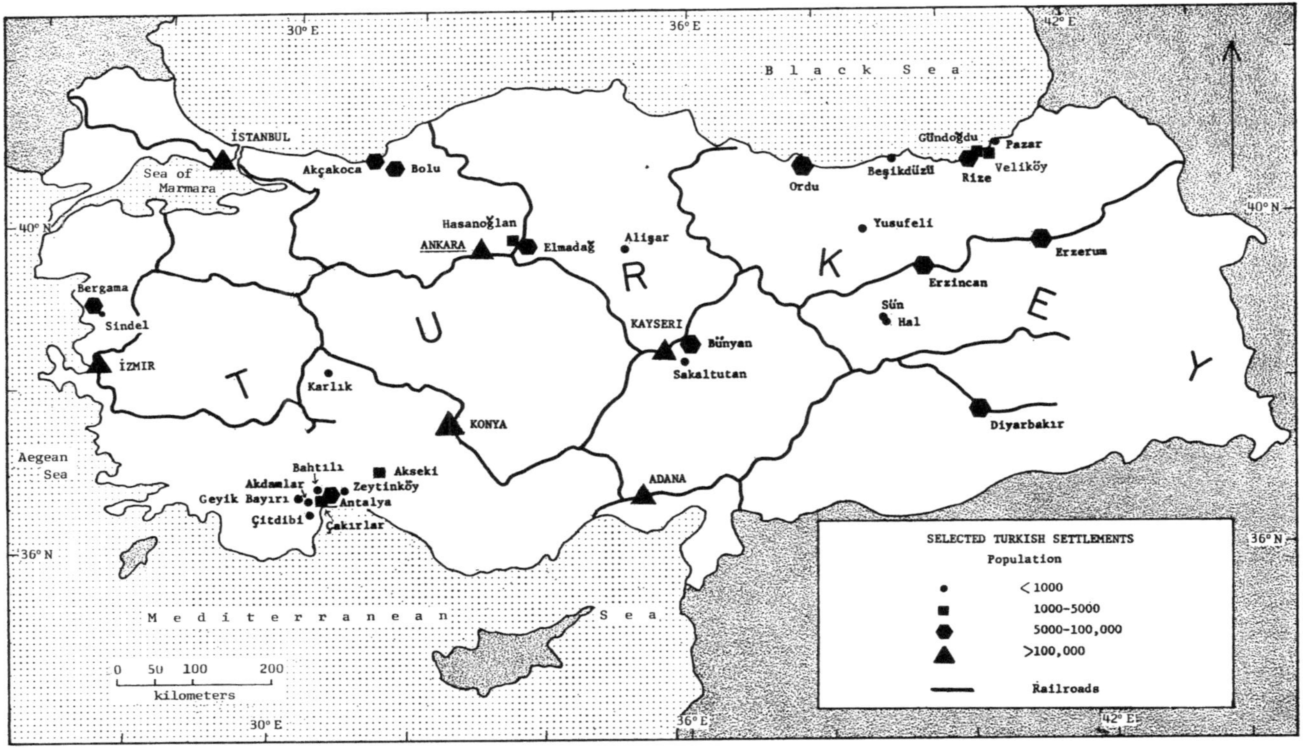

products, the greater is the *actual mobility* of individuals and the greater their *psychological mobility*. People with less contact with modern technology and long-established relatedness to familiar surroundings have less psychological mobility.

Sherif's findings corroborate both of the themes chosen here. The "local conditions" which initially pushed villagers out of both settlements were the limited natural resources rather than the restrictions on village employment opportunity caused by changes in the methods of resource exploitation. (Yet it is often the case that a push does arise from such changes. In a study of farm mechanization on 3,015 Turkish farms, it was found that powerful labour displacement effects were present.[10] The ultimate effects on employment were not completely clear, however, because cultivation was also expanded, causing increases in labour needed for the non-mechanized part of the farm work and for processing and marketing.) Sherif clearly corroborates the other theme, for the village which may be said to have been *urban-directed* successfully transferred labour to the town, whereas the *rural-directed* one did not. This distinction—the one between rural and urban-directedness—helps to explain Sherif's observations and will be used in the typology presented later.

Other kinds of rural studies have been attempted with valuable results. For example Daniel Lerner has studied personality types, classifying individuals as "modern, transitional, and traditional",[11] and Barbara and George Helling have measured the variation among provinces of a number of social and economic indexes.[12] The unique feature of the present study, however, is that small rural communities will be regarded as units having distinctive histories and social processes and will be compared with each other on the basis of information provided in a number of detailed case studies.

The preparation of the typology was initiated by making a preliminary bibliographical survey of community studies. This was used to assess the range and type of materials available without actually classifying their contents in detail. The materials were then read for content while continuing search added considerably to the number of works. These *in toto* became the basis for an initial outline or typology.

Once village types as revealed by specific case studies became apparent, five communities which were the subjects of the most detailed monographs were selected for further investigation. In the summer of 1963, the author and his wife (also a cultural geographer) visited the communities of Alişar, Bahtılı, Hasanoğlan, Sakaltutan, and Sindel with the original studies in hand. This field work gave much needed historical perspective to developments in the villages during the years intervening since the time of the original investigations. The authors of the original studies were also interviewed wherever possible, as were Turkish and foreign government officials, planners, and scholars who might give further insight into the nature of these villages and their environment. A further step was a series of interviews with villagers in which the problem of the nature of economic development at the village level was presented to them in simplified terms and their opinions were solicited. In this way, working within the limits of time and resources available to the investigator, a unique fund of information concerning process and historical development was accumulated.

Next, the results of the five village restudies, the original studies of the same villages, reports on other villages outside the restudy sample, and results of interviews concerning a few of these outside cases were all assembled. The original working typology was then modified and enlarged in light of the new information, and a final version prepared, which is felt to be comprehensive and capable of receiving additional materials, statistical and literary, as they become available.

## Defining the Village Community

It is necessary to define the village community, as that term will be used in the typology. Several possibilities are available. One is to use a criterion of settlement size alone, in which case the usual official divisions are these: a place with less than 2,000 inhabitants is a village (*köy*),[13] a place with 2,000 to 20,000 population is a town (*kasaba*), and one with more than 20,000 is a city (*şehir*).

Another possibility is to accept as villages all those settlements defined as such by their officially designated administrative functions. The smallest political and administrative unit in Turkey is headed by an elected mayor (*muhtar*) and a council of elders (*ihtiyar meclisi*) and is officially designated a village. Its settlement size typically is less than 2,000, but there are instances of places which have grown larger and have not been placed under a municipality (*belediye*) form of local government. Other exceptions occur where the central government's provincial (*vilayet*) or county (*kaza*) administrative offices are situated in very small communities. In such cases the village form of local government is not considered adequate and the municipality form supersedes it. In this way settlements smaller than 2,000 sometimes become known officially as towns or cities rather than villages.

Neither of the foregoing definitions was considered satisfactory for use here. Instead, settlements were accepted into the typology which were any of the following: smaller in size than 2,000 persons; smaller than 2,000 when the initial studies were undertaken, but which had grown larger since then; or were made up of villagers held together by an essentially village culture even though located within an area administratively defined as a town or city. By avoiding the restrictiveness of a purely administrative or size definition of village, it was possible to consider villagers wherever they might be found and thus to gain valuable historical perspective on the whole continuum of change.

## Types of Villages

The typology distinguishes two main groups of villages each of which is subdivided so that altogether a total of seven types is specified. Nineteen villages were distributed among these seven types. The two main groups are distinguished by differences in their frequency and type of contact with urban centres. Thus they may be characterized as urban-directed and rural-directed respectively.

The urban-directed villages display a clear and growing association with larger urban places. The phenomenon is not limited to the environs of the major centres, Istanbul, Ankara, and Izmir, but occurs also in villages whose urban-directedness is toward provincial capitals and even county seats. Insofar as these villages are involved in agricultural production rather than in increasingly important manufacturing and service production, they have *daily* cityward movements of fresh produce in season and of dairy products throughout the year. This distinguishes their agricultural marketing from other settlements whose crops are usually harvested only once a year, marketed infrequently, and dependent for their sale upon intermediary wholesalers and government agencies. The urban-directed settlements may even serve as dormitory suburbs for city wage-earners, whereas those workers who seek work beyond the rural-directed village must detach themselves seasonally in migratory movement patterns. Thus the contrast is between urban-directed villages which are in direct, daily contact with towns and cities and rural-directed ones which are not.[14]

Within each of the two main groups, villages are classified according to different sets of characteristics. Each of the four urban-directed types is a special constellation of income-producing activities, locational proximity to the urban centre, and social organization. Each of the three rural-directed types is related to markets beyond the village in a different way. Thus the subdivisions are based on one set of criteria for the urban-directed villages and another for the rural-directed ones.

TABLE 1: TYPES OF VILLAGES

| *Urban-directed* | *Rural-directed* |
|---|---|
| 1. Shadow | 5. Market-seeking |
| 2. Annexed | 6. Market-recognizing |
| 3. Satellite | 7. Market-ignoring |
| 4. Summer dormitory | |

*Shadow villages*

Peter Suzuki has described neighbourhood clusters of immigrant villagers in the Istanbul area which the present writer chooses to call shadow villages.[15] These geographically discrete groups of village families living in larger cities have no individual administrative existence, but maintain a sense of identity through their common point of origin from somewhere else in Turkey. Economically their life is nearly identical with that of other city dwellers, but it appears that the presence of such groups within larger, urban populations provides a "landing place" for immigrants, thus making the transition to city life easier.[16] Kemal Karpat suggests that such a sense of transplanted "community solidarity" exists only during the transitional stages of immigration, and that once familiarity with the new environment is established and job security assured, such shadow villages may be dissipated.[17]

The shadow village may also be a particular consequence of the specialization of occupational roles sometimes encountered in Turkey. Thus it is said that cooks come from Bolu, businessmen from Akseki, and truck gardeners from the village of Yusufeli. Except for the truck gardeners whose Yusufeli origins have been verified,[18] these examples are only based on impressions; but the important hypothesis remains that many well-defined, if not generally known, channels exist through which villagers can gain new skills and find employment far from home. Suzuki suggests that "... the peasant's attachment to his most meaningful unit of social organization (the village)—deplored by the social scientist because it is felt to militate against socio-economic development is, in this case, operating to promote such development."[19] It is for this reason that shadow villages have been felt important enough for inclusion in this typology.

*Annexed villages*

Annexed villages are those so near to larger urban places that eventually they are engulfed by the physical expansion of the latter. In these cases the village is reclassified as a neighbourhood (*mahalle*) within the city, and finally, with the growth of population, may become either a subdistrict (*nahiye*) or even a seat of county government (*ilçe merkezi*). The earlier official village status of such places can often be identified by the retention of the word for village (*köy*) in their names (e.g. Ortaköy in Istanbul). Another approach is to compare early maps and village lists[20] with recent censuses. Perhaps the most studied of the annexed villages is Balgat, now part of Ankara, which was made famous by Daniel Lerner's parable of "The Grocer and the Chief".[21]

The pattern of life in annexed villages has become essentially urban. Residents commute to other parts of the city for employment. The very few who survive as farmers are anomalies, and produce only special crops such as fresh vegetables. Land values rise rapidly, and house rentals become a source of income for those able to invest in building. Wages are almost always derived from the manufacturing and service sectors of the economy, and prosperity has usually increased significantly.

*Satellite villages*

Satellite villages occupy a geographical situation slightly different from that of annexed villages. These settlements are located beyond the administrative limits of larger urban places (i.e. they are external to the municipality, although they may be in the same county), and are discrete communities in a morphological sense through being surrounded by open countryside. Their association with larger towns and cities is a result of their being located within reasonable commuting distance. The limit of this distance would be within one or two hours by foot or bicycle (perhaps ten kilometres); by bus or train the geographic distance can be greater, although the time separation is usually less.[22] For example, the communities of Hasanoğlan[23] and Elmadağ (Küçükyozgat),[24] east of Ankara, are linked to that city by daily rail service, while Sindel, near Bergama,[25] and Zeytinköy, north-east of Antalya,[26] are within walking distance of those towns.

The sources of income for satellite communities are more varied than those for either annexed villages or rural-directed communities. Thus, when the writer visited Hasanoğlan in August 1963, an estimated 100 workers were commuting daily to Ankara by train, as were a similarly large number from the neighbouring community of Elmadağ (Küçükyozgat). Hasanoğlan is an atypical settlement due to the presence of a Village Institute,[27] but it displays tendencies like those of other satellite villages such as Sindel and Zeytinköy. There is, for example, an emphasis on keeping herds of animals for milk sales to the city as well as for use within the local community. Between 1944, when Yasa compiled his data, and 1963, sheep and goats in Hasanoğlan increased from 5,732 to 7,832 and cows increased from 242 to approximately 600, while oxen (plough animals) decreased from 293 to 200. In the same pattern, milk and firewood are sold almost daily to the citizens of Bergama by the people of Sindel, although in this case milk sales may be declining because of the decline in acreage suitable for grazing. Although traditional agriculture is still practised in this type of village, increases in *per capita* income are associated with urban-directedness and greater reliance on the manufacturing, construction and service sectors of the economy. For example, fifteen to twenty unskilled labourers travel on foot daily from Sindel to Bergama for employment.

### *Summer dormitory villages*

A final, highly specialized type of urban-directed small rural community exists which, so far as this writer's knowledge goes, has not been the subject of research. Such settlements might be called summer dormitory villages, because a substantial part of their income is earned by playing seasonal host to crowds of city folk. The long-established Turkish custom of going to the *yayla*, or summer mountain pasture, during the summer months persists among those city dwellers who can afford it. Today they may as well go to the seashore or other felicitous surroundings. For example, the county seat of Akçakoca on the Black Sea has a great influx of population in the summer, while numerous mountain communities are similarly visited by people from Adana and Ankara.

The full economic and social effects of incursions into the summer dormitory villages is not known, but it may be assumed that the seasonal provision of services and supplies to the vacationers increases local incomes. The infusion of sophisticated urban culture into more traditional areas which may accompany these movements also speeds the processes of social change. The improvement of transportation favours these developments, although it may also reverse fortunes in some instances. For example, mountain villages above the Adana plain which were once popular with wealthy lowlanders are being abandoned in favour of the summer delights of Istanbul, which is now easily accessible by plane, train, and motor.[28] On the other hand, the summer exodus from large cities to the surrounding countryside has also been increased by improved means of travel.

*Rural-directed villages*

The subdivision among rural-directed villages is made according to their different relationships to the external market. The agricultural activities of these villages involve producing crops for local consumption and for sale, and there are gradations in the relative importance of each among villages. The same is true of non-agricultural products. Those settlements whose inhabitants rarely do anything but consume their own production locally may be described as market-ignoring villages. The situation in villages exporting beyond their own limits is more complex.[29] There are some which enter the market economy during good years but which may actually import food if hit by bad conditions, particularly drought. Similar to these villages are others in which an inequitable distribution of land, or an inadequate proportion of land particularly suited for the production of cash crops, results in the use of the market-place by some, but not all, members of the community. Conditions in such villages are extremely varied, but all of them may be subsumed under the term market-recognizing villages. A third and final subtype has been identified in which a rapid and continuing change to cash crops has not yet reached its environmental limits and thereby exhausted local opportunities for development. Settlements of this type have been termed market-seeking villages.

It is not only the resource endowment of each village's area that is important, but also the position occupied by the village in a historical continuum of development and change. Fifty years ago many more Turkish villages could have been classified as market-ignoring than can be so classified today. For example, the villages of Bahtılı and Çakırlar, described by the present author, have since the first World War changed to a market-seeking status;[30] while Alişar, though linked to the world by improved transportation, still lingers in the market-recognizing class.[31]

Four prerequisites to agricultural development at the village level must therefore be recognized. They are: (1) the development of a market and marketing system exterior to the village; (2) the development of transportation linking the village to the marketing system; (3) sufficient resource potential and incentive for change at the village level; and (4) a mechanism by which necessary urban-derived inputs, such as credit and new equipment, may reach the village.

### *Market-ignoring villages*

Market-ignoring villages can be divided generally into those which have a potential for change but lag behind for other reasons, and those which are so poorly endowed with natural resources that significant positive changes appear impossible even within the extended limits of modern technology. Examples of the first type would be the many grain-farming villages of the plateau which, when eventually supplied with irrigation water and better roads, may some day switch their production to crops like sugar beets. Examples of the second type are numerous mountain and forest villages located on slopes so steep and with soils so poor that they cannot be improved and might better be removed from production. Hayri Nuray estimates the proportion of all villagers occupying such marginal areas in or near forests at 37·7 per cent of the total population, with the proportion by province ranging from 72·8 per cent in Kastamonu to 15·9 per cent in Erzurum.[32] This figure, however, seems unusually large and a more realistic one of 22·3 per cent of the Turkish population can be derived from the 1960 census of population.[33] Where hardships are extreme, it is possible that voluntary depopulation of some villages will occur in response to increasing urban opportunities.

In market-ignoring villages no crop surplus occurs, and the natural environment in many such places is literally not suited for cash crops. *Per capita* incomes in these communities are stabilized at a very low level, or are declining, either because of depletion of resources or because of increases in population without attendant production increases, or both. To survive, men and sometimes even women and children seek employment elsewhere on a seasonal basis, or longer. An example of such a community with a stable or slowly declining *per capita* income would be the village subdivision (*mahalle*) of Geyik Bayırı in the Bey Mountains west of Antalya;[34] while two examples of mountain villages with rapidly declining *per capita* incomes derived from local sources are Çitdibi near Geyik Bayırı[35] and Hal in Elazığ Province.[36] In the two latter villages emigration, both seasonal and longer-term, is becoming increasingly important.

### *Market-recognizing villages*

The wide variety of market-recognizing villages requires special consideration. At least three significant variations occur within this subcategory. They are: those communities occasionally marketing surpluses of subsistence crops, usually grains; those producing limited amounts of cash crops; and those where an unevenly distributed control of available resources results in a saleable surplus for some, but not all, of the people concerned. In the latter case village income is inequitably distributed among the inhabitants or between the inhabitants and absentee landlords. The unsatisfactory distribution of income does not necessarily go hand in hand with an inadequate development of the area's natural resources. For example, cotton farms in the Çukurova are often worked by poor tenants whose efforts provide absentee owners with ample returns per hectare of land.[37] Yet, in such cases, the contribution of the village as a productive whole to the market economy may be far above average, while the lot of its own workers more closely resembles the poor conditions in market-ignoring communities. Thus, social and economic development are not always correlated positively.

The Black Sea region east of Ordu is an excellent example of an area producing limited amounts of cash crops. In the eastern half of the region, around Rize, where conditions of humidity, temperature, and altitude are favourable, tea is the important crop.[38] To the west, hazelnuts are favoured by the environment and supplant tea in importance.[39] In both cases, only limited areas within the optimum environmental zone are suitable for the cultivation of these crops, for in addition to climatic factors, soil, water, and slope also restrict production. Tunçdilek reports that "at least 75 per cent of the houses in the Black Sea region were built in an area where subsistence agriculture prevails".[40] This is emphasized by the Hellings' report, which places Rize Province among those with the lowest level of living and the highest number of migrant workers in Turkey.[41] On the other hand, where tea has been introduced amazing changes are taking place. Tunçdilek states that during the last five to ten years emigration from those villages where tea production has increased has "completely stopped".[42] In such places an annual profit of 1,000 TL per decare (about $450 per acre) can be realized.[43] Local production of subsistence crops has declined. For example, in the village of Veliköy where once only two or three families purchased grain outside the settlement, now all 180 families do so.[44] Planhol reports a similarly unequal distribution among farms producing hazelnuts. In the limited areas where the crop can be raised, the usual gross income from a farmer's harvest ranges from approximately 4,500 to 9,000 TL ($500–$1,000).[45] Hazelnut villages are also marked by a diminishing dependence upon maize and an increasing use of wheat flour.[46]

Sherif's least isolated village, Beşikdüzü, now the headquarters of a county subdistrict in Trabzon Province, is another example of a market-recognizing settlement. According to Sherif, external contacts associated with the hazelnut trade provide a communication channel, and the scarcity of tillable land acts as a push to introduce people to other areas and to the way of getting there. For some, this has created a desire to migrate.[47] Thus, the inhabitants of such settlements recognize markets but do not all share equally in their use. The recent introduction of tea into this area may alter things still further.[48]

A slightly different example of the market-recognizing type of settlement is Akdamlar Mahalle of Geyik Bayırı village. In this settlement citrus fruit is produced wherever slope, soil, and irrigation water permit, but production is severely restricted by the scarcity of suitable land.[49] Again, the market provides limited cash income for certain farmers, but the village as a productive whole remains near the subsistence level.

Another major variation among market-recognizing villages is found in those which produce occasional surpluses of subsistence crops such as grain. These are probably the most numerous of all villages in Anatolia.[50] Much could be said of these villages, but for this typology it is only important to observe that they depend heavily upon grains, that the share of their total output attributable to livestock is falling,[51] and that village prosperity depends upon favourable climatic conditions which are very uncertain.[52] This dependence on grains, and the wide variation from year to year in the amount available either for consumption or sale, is evident in the village of Sün near Elazığ.[53] Here, cotton, barley, and vegetables are grown, but wheat is by far the most important crop, while herding is disappearing due to a shortage of pasture. The amount of grain sold beyond the settlement varies from 15 to 100 tons per year. Thus the market orientation of Sün varies with the clemency of the weather. Morrison's village of Alişar[54] and Stirling's village of Sakaltutan[55] apparently experience similar variations. It is also likely that the village of Karlık, described by Sherif as his most isolated settlement,[56] is in this category, although he did not report details of agricultural production.

The relation between climate and prosperity cannot be analysed in detail in this typology, but the complexities involved should be noted in passing. Simple correlations between annual rainfall and annual cereal production for the wheat-producing region will provide some information, but a fuller understanding of seasonal and other relationships is needed. Table 2 shows the sequence of environmental events, human responses, and ensuing results as they might occur in an Anatolian grain-producing village. Only one type of situation has

TABLE 2: AGRICULTURAL SEQUENCE (SIMPLIFIED) IN AN ANATOLIAN WHEAT PRODUCING VILLAGE

(Assumes abundant fallow)

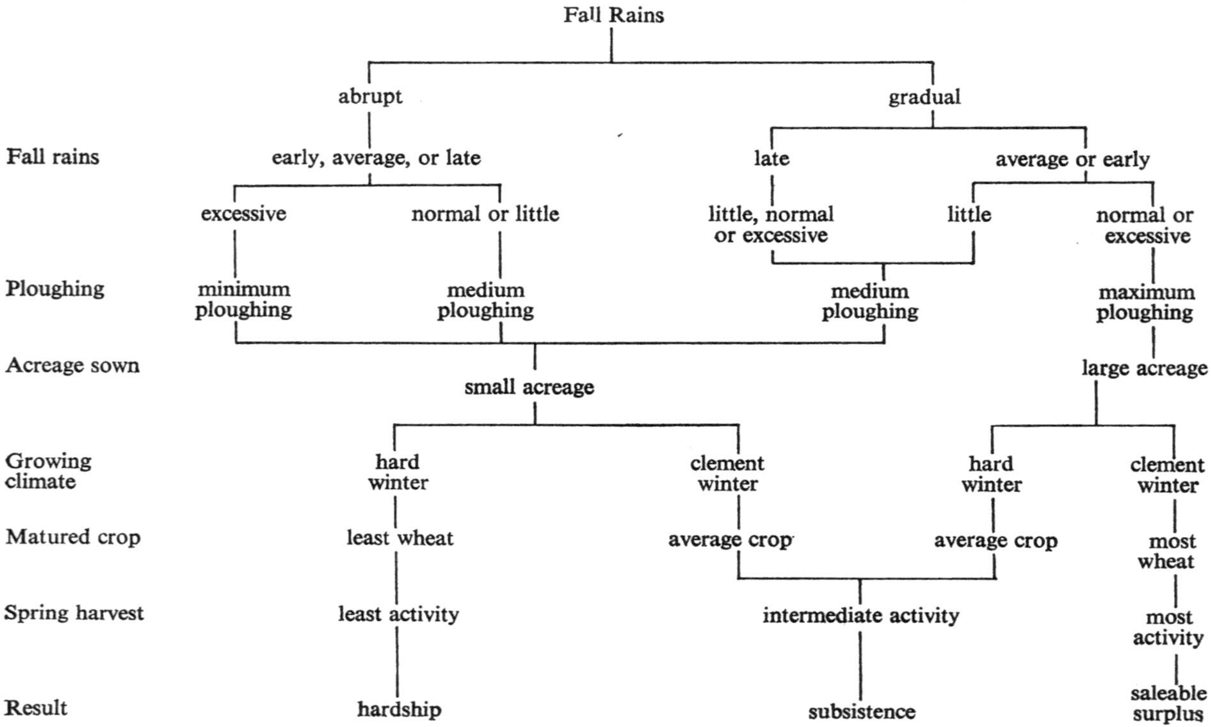

been diagrammed, that in which abundant fallow and unlimited property are assumed. In the much more likely event of limited land holdings, and hence probably inadequate fallow as well, yields would be lower. By following the flow lines in the diagram different sequences of events can be traced to their conclusions. When this diagram is considered along with our knowledge of the variability of Turkish climate,[57] the uncertainties of market participation by this type of village can be appreciated.

*Market-seeking villages*

The market-seeking villages incorporate the pattern of livelihood activities described for market-recognizing communities in many ways. Less need be said, therefore, about this type. Its major distinction is that its abundant local resources allow a continuing expansion of the areas devoted to cash crops. This usually permits incomes to rise generally throughout the community, at least for a while. In other words, the cash crop potential has yet to be fully exploited. Such a situation is found in Veliköy and in Bahtılı, near Antalya. In the latter settlement the introduction of commercial citrus in conjunction with the existence of abundant land suitable for the crop is bringing a high level of prosperity to most of its inhabitants.[58] Other possibilities for exceptional prosperity may be found when a village masters the production of a craft product,[59] or attracts some profitable local industry.[60]

The market-seeking communities show many signs of losing their strictly village status and becoming what will be described below as incipient towns. Their increased agricultural incomes have generated sufficient demands for town services to move some of those services to the village. For example, in 1961 the only non-agricultural establishment in Bahtılı besides its two coffee-houses was a small sawmill. In the summer of 1963 the author also found a grocer, a barber, a tailor, and a peanut wholesaler. While these people were dependent for much of their prosperity upon profits from cash crops raised within the boundaries of the settlement, they were now doing town types of business and attracting additional custom from beyond the village limits. Bahtılı is thus slowly increasing its total prosperity through non-agricultural as well as agricultural means. In keeping with this expansion of economic opportunity, emigration from prosperous villages such as Bahtılı is small. In fact, such villages often attract migratory labour on a seasonal basis.

TABLE 3: SUMMARY OF THE VILLAGE TYPOLOGY

| *Characteristics of villages* | URBAN-DIRECTED | | | | RURAL-DIRECTED | | |
|---|---|---|---|---|---|---|---|
| | *Shadow* | *Annexed* | *Satellite* | *Summer dormitory* | *Market-seeking* | *Market-recognizing* | *Market-ignoring* |
| Population movement | Strong inward | Medium inward | Small inward | Variable | Small outward or zero | Medium outward | Strong outward |
| *Per capita* income trend | upward | upward | upward | seasonally unstable | upward | unstable | stable or declining |
| Sources of external earnings | wage earners | wage earners, some fresh produce | wage commuters and fresh produce | seasonal visitors (rentals, personal services, fresh produce) | crafts and cash crops | crafts, cash crops, surplus subsistence crops | none (no crop surplus) |
| Development potential | prosperity linked to manufacturing, construction and service sectors | | | prosperity varies with fads and transport cost | cash crop potential unsaturated | cash crop potential saturated and/or unequitably distributed | no cash crop potential |
| Cases | Istanbul neighbourhoods (Suzuki) | Balgat | Hasanoğlan<br>Sindel<br>Elmadağ<br>Zeytinköy | Akçakoça | Bahtılı<br>Bünyan<br>Veliköy<br>Gündoğdu | Akdamlar<br>Alişar<br>Sakaltutan<br>Beşikdüzü<br>Sün<br>Karlık (?) | Geyik Bayırı<br>Hal |

## Paths of Development

The yielding of subsistence agriculture to cash crops and the growing involvement of small communities with larger urban places are the two interdependent historical sequences found in the lives of most villages. It would be a mistake, however, to conclude that all villages experience precisely the same development process. The typology has shown that there is no single typical village or villager. Its seven types characterize the variety which research has already disclosed, and further research may well suggest that an even more diversified typology would be appropriate. Similarly, the change in these villages over time follows several different paths rather than a single chain of events which is inevitably repeated by each community in its turn.

At least three paths may be distinguished according to their immediate, although presumably not final, destinations. One is a path which might be termed *urban capture*, signifying the eventual engulfing of the village in an urban complex. The second is a path of *rural transformation*, signifying the participation of a village in technological advance and other improvements, but its retention of an agrarian orientation. The third is a path which leads to becoming a town in its own right, a condition which is heralded by becoming an *incipient town*. None of these destinations can be considered final, except perhaps the first, which would be attained as urban culture spread over large areas capturing all before it, but only in the very long run. Within the foreseeable future of the villages studied here, however, the three different destinations are apparent and it is these which should guide present planning and thought.

### *Urban capture*

Practically all the villages which become subject to urban capture have been rural-directed at some time in the past. The only exceptions would be a few places located near the great administrative centres such as Istanbul, which have had an urban-directedness through long periods of history. Normally, however, the village begins by being market-ignoring and then progresses up a ladder which leads through one or more intervening types, including an urban-directed stage. The pivotal events are that some nearby town should exist and grow, and that there also be improvements in transportation. Then the urban area's physical and psychological outreach, as well as its attraction of labour, products, and services from the village community, increases. It is not necessary that the village community should pass through all the marketing types (5 and 6) or that it pass through every one of the urban-directed conditions (1 to 4), but some of these types will certainly be experienced along the way.

An example of a village whose eventual destination may be urban capture is Sindel, located six kilometres south and east of the city of Bergama.[61] Sindel's population in 1960 was 287, an increase of 61 over the 1950 census figure. The village is built on stony slopes covered with maquis which rise to the south, while to the north lies an alluvial valley with Bergama easily in view across the flat terrain. Of 648 hectares of village land, 236 are in fields and pasture, but of these only 54 hectares are owned by the villagers themselves. Grains are raised for local consumption, and some cotton and tobacco are grown. There is a severe shortage of land brought on by the large (percentage) population increase and the withdrawal of adjacent alluvial lands into personal commercial management by owners located in Bergama.

Sindel has some of the characteristics of a market-recognizing village, but in this functional classification an important new development warrants placing Sindel in the urban-directed category. An increasing number of villagers are now turning to the nearby town of Bergama for additional income. At the same time, Bergama itself is growing rapidly and will inevitably expand its borders geographically. While the intervening farm lands present a barrier to city expansion toward Sindel, it is not inconceivable that the city will eventually engulf the village. Further impetus in that direction is provided by a textile mill which has been located on the road connecting Bergama and Sindel. Meanwhile, the close proximity of the two actually acts as a deterrent to the establishment of urban-type enterprises within the village. Thus, Sindel's development path could bypass the independent stage of the incipient town and proceed straight to urban capture.

### *Rural transformation*

For most of Turkey's villages, economic progress has come through rural transformation, at least initially. Originally nearly self-sufficient, the villages gradually fall under the influence of growing urban markets and improved systems of transportation, but all at a distance too great for daily commuting. Concurrently, new ideas concerning the techniques of agronomy, marketing, and financing spread and are given a trial. If the local resource base permits a favourable agricultural response, it is likely to be forthcoming. In that case, the shift towards cash crops proceeds, and a stronger market orientation results.

On the other hand, the village may not be able to respond, and population increments will be induced to migrate more or less permanently. Some village communities will be passed over in the course of national development simply because their natural resources (possibly including the people themselves) were not appropriately constituted or located.

An example of a village community which has already proceeded far along the path of rural transformation is Bahtılı. Bahtılı occupies a portion of the fertile alluvial valley of the Boğa Çay approximately fifteen kilometres west of the city of Antalya. Its population was 673 in 1960. Within the boundaries of Bahtılı are 600 hectares of cultivated land, forty-four per cent of which was under irrigation in 1960. In addition there are perhaps another 200 hectares of wasteland and riverbed within the settlement. The population in 1960 was divided into 122 households of which 120 owned one or more hectares of land. None of these farms occupies territory as rocky and inhospitable as the majority of the fields in Sindel. Maize and other grains were grown on forty per cent of the arable land, and peanuts on another sixteen per cent. Early spring vegetables destined for major urban markets in the north were grown on ten per cent of the land, and the remaining thirty-four per cent was devoted to the production of citrus. Livelihood activities in Bahtılı are chiefly agricultural, but the entire situation is being changed by a substitution of the cash crops for subsistence crops. Even though orchard expansion is alternately restricted by the rising cost and declining amount of unappropriated irrigation water, the switch from grains to citrus continues unabated. When the writer returned to the village in 1963, he found an additional 80 hectares of land given over to citrus seedlings, making a total commitment to this crop of nearly forty-seven per cent of the total farmland available.

New crops have added significantly to the income of villagers. Where maize from a decare of land was worth about 125 TL ($14) at 1960 prices, green beans brought nearly 1,000 TL ($110) and oranges 1,600 TL ($177). Much of the new income finds its way into house construction, but since 1960 Bahtılı has begun to discover other outlets for its money. The villagers have already made a 6,000 TL ($670) deposit toward the maintenance of a new system of piped water which will be installed by the government. In conjunction with all this prosperity, non-agricultural services like those previously described are being attracted to the village. Few of its residents now show any inclination to leave the village for work in Ankara, Istanbul, or West Germany. Bahtılı, therefore, has experienced a rural transformation based on the introduction of new crops, and while it promises to remain essentially an agricultural community, its future should be far different from its past.

*Incipient towns*

As income increases, and sources diversify through the addition of service establishments, industries, and official administrative functions, a village may become an incipient town and undergo urbanization in its own right. Villages which evolve along this path have usually exceeded 2,000 persons in size. Agriculture typically continues to be significant, but barbers, tailors, butchers, cobblers, grocers, restaurants, government offices, and banks become conspicuous and begin to serve not only local customers but those from beyond the community's boundaries. Incipient towns often appear to owe much of their growth to their being assigned higher administrative functions in the national administrative hierarchy. New income-producing activity introduced in this way from the outside has a multiplier effect on the local economy through its demand for local inputs and the respending of incomes which are newly generated. Prior to entering upon this expanded stage, towns may have been either rural- or urban-directed; the steps along the way are not uniform. The destination itself is likely to be achieved by an increasing number of Turkey's present rural communities as the entire nation grows in population, economic size, and the scale of government administrative activity.

*Planning for the development of rural Turkey*

Because Turkey's villagers live in many types of communities, and because these communities are experiencing several different patterns of change, it follows that what is best for one settlement may not be best for another. Government policies which aim at assisting rural development will need to be adapted to widely varying situations and possibilities for advance. The future prosperity of every villager does not necessarily depend upon his community's becoming an incipient town, being integrated within an urban complex, or undergoing rural transformation. Neither does it depend upon the villager's detaching himself from rural life and migrating to one of the great cities or to a job in Western Europe. However, each villager's prospect does depend upon at least one of these things. Such is the variety with which planners for the welfare of Turkey's rural majority must deal.

Furthermore, the differences among communities suggest that a strategy of development might be adopted which gives minimal help to those which are already developing rapidly and concentrates instead on those cases showing good potential but where external stimuli are most needed. Such a strategy would give primary support to the rural-directed settlements, but not to all of them, since many already are well along in the rural transformation. Another basis for the strategy would be to encourage the growth of urban-directed villages indirectly through town and city development programmes. The latter would have to be planned together with the development of the rural settlements within their range of influence. Similarly, the conversion of rural settlements into incipient towns through the opening of government offices, strategically chosen so as to maximize the total stimulus on surrounding rural areas, would be another promising possibility. These means of improving the welfare of rural people all merit trial and continuing study. Meanwhile, Turkey's situation, dynamic and troubled, heightens the need for answers.

NOTES

1. For a critical review of these studies through 1960 see John F. Kolars, "Community Studies in Rural Turkey", *Annals of the Association of American Geographers*, Vol. 52, No. 4 (December 1962), pp. 476–89.

2. The most comprehensive of such surveys is the "Rural Development Research Project" conducted by the Social Planning Division of the Turkish State Planning Organization in co-operation with the United States' AID Mission in Ankara. While the final results of this survey have yet to become available, a summary of the methodology employed may be found in Frederick W. Frey, "Surveying Peasant Attitudes in Turkey", *The Public Opinion Quarterly*, Vol. 27, No. 3 (Fall, 1963), pp. 335–55.

An additional survey conducted under the direction of Ruşen Keleş and Orhan Türkay during the summer of 1961, *Köylü Gözü ile Türk Köylerinde İktisadı ve Toplumsal Değişme*, Türk İktisadi Gelişmesi Araştırma Projesi No. 13, Siyasal Bilgiler Fakültesi, Maliye Enstitüsü (Ankara: Yılmazoğlu Modern Teksir ve Fotokopi, 1962), examines the nature of change in forty-four widely scattered rural Turkish communities. Its chronological presentation of the introduction into the villages of various elements of change gives additional value to the data. The survey also presents in tabulated form what the villagers believe to be the reasons for the observed changes. However, this survey thus does not distinguish specific village types, but rather shows the importance of change in Turkish villages as a whole.

3. George M. Foster, *Traditional Cultures: and the Impact of Technological Change* (New York: Harper and Brothers, 1962), p. 29.

4. *Ibid.*, p. 31.

5. *Ibid.*, pp. 31–4.

6. For the purpòses of this study "cash crops" are defined as those crops specifically grown for sale outside the village rather than for local consumption, and which in the absence of an external market would either be lacking or grown in insignificant quantities within the village. Sugar beets are an example of a crop which would not be grown at all if the opportunity for external sales were lacking; oranges are an example of a crop which—where natural conditions allowed—would be grown for local consumption even though no external market existed, *but in negligible quantities*. "Traditional" or "subsistence" crops are those which constitute the staples of the village diet. Wheat is the best example and is grown nearly everywhere in Turkey. Obviously surpluses of "subsistence" crops can be and are sold on the market external to the village, but unlike "cash" crops their level of production is only peripherally influenced by external stimuli.

7. Frederic C. Shorter, "Growth and Basic Structural Change in Turkey", Research Paper No. 1964 (1) of the Princeton Program in Near Eastern Studies (Princeton: January 1964), pp. 9–10 and 25.

8. John F. Kolars, *Tradition, Season, and Change in a Turkish Village*, Department of Geography Research Paper No. 82 (Chicago: University of Chicago Press, 1963), pp. 198–200.

9. Muzaffer Sherif, "Differential Contact with Modern Technology in Five Turkish Villages", *An Outline of Social Psychology*, Revised ed. (New York: Harper and Brothers, 1956), pp. 692–701. Material in brackets added.

10. Siyasal Bilgiler Fakültesi, *Türkiye'de Zirai Makinalaşma*, Ankara Üniversitesi S.B.F. Yayınları No. 39–21 (Ankara, 1954).

11. Daniel Lerner, *The Passing of Traditional Society* (Glencoe, Illinois: The Free Press, 1958).

12. Barbara and George Helling, *Rural Turkey—A New Socio-Statistical Appraisal*, İstanbul Üniversitesi Yayınları No. 795 (İstanbul: Fakülteler Matbaası, 1958).

13. Subdivisions or neighbourhoods within villages and towns are called *mahalle*. Settlements smaller than villages have a variety of names in Turkish (e.g. *kom, oba, divan, mezraa*), but the latter are not officially recognized as political subdivisions in the way that villages are. See Ali Tanoğlu, "The Geography of Settlement", *Review of the Geographical Institute of the University of Istanbul*, International Edition, No. 1 (1954), pp. 3–27.

14. While this discussion is phrased primarily in economic terms, a number of related questions dealing with the political and sociological aspects of such contacts may be asked. For example: At what frequency of contact does a significant diffusion of new ideas occur, and does the level of conservatism vary enough from city to city to produce significant differences in the quality of rural-urban contacts?

15. Peter Suzuki, "Village Solidarity among Turkish Peasants Undergoing Urbanization", *Science*, Vol. 132, No. 3431 (September 30, 1960), pp. 891–2; and in conversation with P. S.

16. In much the same way, people from villages near the city of Antalya patronize city grocers and shopkeepers related by blood or marriage to some member of the village. Such establishments become way-stations for villagers visiting the town.

17. Suggested to the author in a seminar at Princeton, February 13, 1964.

18. Jack R. Harlan, "The Wandering Gardeners of Yusufeli", *Seed World* (April 21, 1950).

19. Suzuki, *op. cit.*, p. 892.

20. For example, see: Türk Cumhuriyeti, Dahiliye Vekâleti, Mahalli İdareler, Umum Müdürlüğü, *Köylerimiz* (İstanbul: Matbaacılık ve Neşriyat Türk Anonim Şirketi, 1939); and Istanbul Belediyesi, *İstanbul Şehri Rehberi* (İstanbul: Matbaacılık ve Neşriyat T.A.Ş., 1934).

21. Lerner, *op. cit.*, chap. 1.

22. According to the 1960 Census of Turkey, only 3·1 per cent of all villages are within ten kilometres of provincial capitals. They contain 4·7 per cent of the total village population. Türk Cumhuriyeti, Başbakanlık, Devlet İstatistik Enstitüsü, *Köyler İstatistiği*, Yayın No. 451 (Ankara: Devlet İstatistiği Enstitüsü Matbaası, 1961), p. 71.

23. Ibrahim Yasa, *Hasanoğlan*, Public Administration Institute for Turkey and the Middle East (Ankara: Yeni Matbaa, 1957).

24. Alâettin Guleç, *Kücükyozgat Köyü*, Ankara Halkevi Neşriyatı (Ankara: Ulus Basımevi, 1937).

25. Ibrahim Yasa, *Sindel Köyü'nün Toplumsal ve Ekonomik Yapısı*, Türkiye ve Orta Doğu Amme İdaresi Enstitüsü Yayınları (Ankara: Balkanoğlu Matbaacılık Ltd., Şti., 1960).

26. Xavier de Planhol, *De la Plaine Pamphylienne aux Lacs Pisidiens: Nomadisme et Vie Paysanne*, Bibliothèque Archeologique et Historique de l'Institute Française d'Archeologie d'Istanbul III (Paris: Librairie Adrien-Maisonneuve, 1958), pp. 369–70.

27. This fact is somewhat obscured in the official, published census of population which includes 695 students enrolled at the Village Institute along with 2,303 regular inhabitants.

28. Communication from Maxwell Berry, former American Vicc-Consul, Adana.

29. Nearly every rural-directed village in Turkey produces most of its own food regardless of whatever else it may sell to the world beyond its boundaries. See Erol Tümertekin, "The Structure of Agriculture in Turkey", *Review of the Geographical Institute of the University of Istanbul*, International Edition, No. 5 (1959), p. 87.

30. Kolars, *Tradition, Season, and Change, op. cit.*, chap. x.

31. John A. Morrison, *Alişar: A Unit of Land Occupance in the Kanak Su Basin of Central Anatolia* (Chicago: University of Chicago Libraries, private edition, 1939), p. 102. In a visit to Alişar in 1963 the present writer found that the same limited sale of grains as described by Morrison thirty-one years earlier constituted the primary export product of the community. This, despite a new all-weather road less than a kilometre away.

32. Hayri Nuray, "Orman İçi Köylerde İskân Meselesi", *V. İskân ve Şehircilik Haftası Konferansları*, Ankara Üniversitesi Siyasal Bilgiler Fakültesi Yayınları No. 139–121 (Ankara: Sevinç Matbaası, 1962), p. 61.

33. *Köyler İstatistiği, op. cit.*, p. 5.

34. Kolars, *Tradition, Season, and Change, op. cit.*, pp. 121–6.

35. *Ibid.*, p. 35, Table 3.

36. Nermin Erdentuğ, *Hal Köyünün Etnolojik Tetkiki*, Ankara Üniversitesi Dil ve Tarih-Coğrafa Fakültesi Yayınları No. 109 (Ankara: Türk Tarih Kurumu Basımevi, 1956), pp. 7–9.

37. John Hiltner, Jr., "An Analysis of the Contemporary Geography of the Çukurova" (unpublished Ph.D. dissertation, Department of Geography, Northwestern University, 1958).

38. Necdet Tunçdilek, "Tea Growing in Turkey", *Review of the Geographical Institute of the University of Istanbul*, International Edition, No. 7 (1961), pp. 53–74; and by the same author, "Observation on Rural Settlement in Two Different Regions of Turkey", *ibid.*, No. 8 (1962), pp. 47–56.

39. Xavier de Planhol, "A travers les chaines pontiques: Plantations cotières et vie montagnarde", Extrait, *Bulletin de l'Association de Geographes Français* (1963), pp. 2–12.

40. Tunçdilek, "Observation on Rural Settlement . . . ", *op. cit.*, p. 50.

41. Ann and George Helling, *op. cit.*, Map 22 and Map 24.

42. Tunçdilek, "Tea Growing . . . ", *op. cit.*, p. 64.

43. *Ibid.*, p. 65.

44. *Ibid.*, p. 63. Veliköy has passed through the market-recognizing type and become a market-seeking village and is so classified below.

45. Planhol, "A travers les chaines pontiques . . . ," *op. cit.*, p. 6. X. P.'s figures have been converted at the rates of 5 NF equal $1.00; and $1.00 equals 9·0 TL.

46. *Ibid.*, p. 4.

47. Sherif, *op. cit.*, p. 696.

48. Tunçdilek, "Tea Growing . . . ," *op. cit.*, Table 1, p. 57.

49. Kolars, *Tradition, Season, and Change, op. cit.*, pp. 120–1.

50. Nicholas Helburn, "A Stereotype of Agriculture in Semi-arid Turkey", *Geographical Review*, Vol. 45 (1955), pp. 375–84.

51. Quentin M. West, "Agricultural Development in Turkey", Foreign Agricultural Service, U.S. Department of Agriculture, Foreign Agriculture Report No. 106 (January 1958), p. 30; and Eva and Abraham Hirsch, "Changes in Agricultural Output Per Capita of Rural Population in Turkey, 1927–1960", *Economic Development and Cultural Change*, Vol. XI, No. 4 (July 1963), pp. 381–4.

52. West, *op. cit.*, *in toto;* and Hirsch, *op. cit.*, *in toto*, serve to illustrate the problem.

53. Erdentuğ, *Sün Köyünün Etholojik Tetkiki*, Ankara Üniversitesi ve Tarih-Coğrafya Fakültesi Yayınları, No. 132 (Ankara: Ayyıldız Matbaası, 1959), pp. 5–6.

54. Morrison, *Alişar*, *op. cit.*

55. Paul Stirling, *Turkish Village* (London: Weidenfeld and Nicolson, 1965), chaps. 4 and 5.

56. Sherif, *op. cit.*, pp. 693–6.

57. Sirri Erinç, "Regional and Seasonal Distribution of Climatic Elements in Turkey and its Dynamic-Genetic Background", *Review of the Geographical Institute of the University of Istanbul*, International Edition, No. 5 (1959), pp. 50–60.

58. Kolars, *Tradition, Season, and Change*, chap. x.

59. An investigtion of Bünyan in Kayseri Province, a community famous for its carpets, might reveal such a situation. However, according to the 1960 Census of Turkey only twelve villages have cottage industries and handicrafts as their main source of income (*Köyler İstatistiği*, *op. cit.*, p. 24).

60. Tunçdilek cites the prosperity of Gündoğdu and Pazar on the Black Sea coast as dependent upon small shipbuilding establishments ("Observation on Rural Settlement . . . ," *op. cit.*, p. 51). He also describes the importance of tea packing to settlements of the Rize area ("Tea Growing", *op. cit.*, pp. 67–8).

61. All data in the discussion of Sindel and Bahtılı are taken from either Kolars, *Tradition, Season, and Change*, *op. cit.;* the 1950, 1955, and 1960 *Census of Population;* or were collected by the author in the summer of 1963.

CHAPTER 5

# Development of the Financial System

*by Oktay Yenal*

THE two decades since the Second World War have witnessed all around the world an unprecedented interest in the economic development and prospects of the poor countries. This interest has encouraged a lively discussion of the determinants of economic growth, producing a voluminous literature and putting its mark on national and international policies. In this preoccupation of theoreticians and strategists, one of the most neglected subjects, in thought as well as in deed, has been the financial aspect of economic development. In fact, as is evidenced by the nature of recent development models—of abstract analysis as well as for actual planning—most theorizing on and implementation of development policies proceeds in terms of the real aspects of economic growth, and emphasizes the changes in real magnitudes. The discussions usually centre around such concepts as the rate of growth, real capital formation, capital-output coefficients and investment criteria. Even when people speak about "financing economic development"—a frequently discussed topic—the issues taken up are more often than not problems of taxation and foreign aid rather than the repercussions of monetary and financial policy on resource allocation and the interactions between the development of a financial superstructure and economic development.[1]

In general, this attitude can be justified: both the final ends and the ultimate costs of development are real (as opposed to financial) phenomena; financial institutions and transactions are mere intermediaries, not ends in themselves for the society. What is more, finance has traditionally been associated, particularly in the industrialized capitalist economies, with the question of economic stability rather than with the problem of growth. Thus, money and finance are easily ignored in worrying about the underdeveloped economies where growth has a decided priority over stability. Accordingly, the tendency of development economists and of the actual policy makers and planners has been to aggregate and net financial transactions and deal with the real variables of the growth process in their analyses. Finance is, of course, not altogether neglected. However, it is often the case that the policy-makers, after paying lip service to the problems relating to the financial system, concern themselves almost exclusively with the ultimate sources and the final uses of resources. In this context all intermediary accounts disappear. In one sense, the simple assumption seems to be that for a development strategy, if we know whom to tax and where to invest, there is not much point in going through the labyrinth of finance. The only significant financial consideration could be whether inflation should be introduced as an alternative to taxation, as in discussions on deficit financing, or whether price stability is compatible with growth as in the monetarist-structuralist controversy.[2] But even in these cases, what is analysed is the impact of financial policies on real variables in the short run rather than the implications of the development of financial superstructure.

This simplification, which is useful in many instances, and particularly as a first approximation, becomes misleading if pursued too far. In an economy where financial development has reached a stage beyond the subsistence or barter economy—and where economic activities are not totally collectivized—the financial structure is an important part of the economic organization, and monetary and other financial transactions have sizable impacts on the real course of events. Therefore, it does not seem just to put financial organization and policy into a somewhat secondary category of the determinants of growth, as is implied in a United Nations report: "Good financial organization cannot by itself produce development; bad financial organization can hamper it."[3] It should by now be clear to the strategists of economic development that no single positive factor can *by itself* produce development and that almost every single negative factor can by itself hamper development—a simple truth following from the fact that economic development is the product of factors which are less than perfectly substitutable. It is therefore of interest to see how improvements in financial organization and policy can contribute to economic development as well as to observe how bad financial management can hamper it at the margin.

Although the importance of the financial aspects of development and the relative neglect of the subject are here stressed by way of introduction, the objective of this paper is not to seek answers to general questions on the relationship between the financial structure and economic growth,[4] but, more modestly, to provide a case study of the Turkish experience. In what follows, the developments in the financial structure of the Turkish economy during the three decades before 1962 will be analysed, and some implications of the findings for future policy will be discussed.

The financial structure of an economy is characterized by the composition of financial assets and the pattern of financial organization. Broadly defined, financial assets are all the intangible assets in the economy. For practical purposes, this definition is narrowed to mean institutionalized intangible assets. Even then, it is not watertight, since the book accounts of business firms could come under the institutional category but would be difficult to quantify. For our purposes, financial assets will mean currency, deposits, securities, and life insurance and pensions claims. The magnitudes of these financial assets as held by the non-bank public are shown in Table 1. Existing data about bonds and stocks are incomplete, and the insurance claims pose problems of valuation. Because of these drawbacks, Table 1 should be taken as no more than a rough picture of the financial asset structure in Turkey.

TABLE 1: FINANCIAL ASSETS HELD BY THE NON-BANK PUBLIC, END OF 1962

| | *Million T.L.* | *Per cent of total* |
|---|---|---|
| Currency and Deposits | *13,015* | 74 |
| 1. Coins | 159 | |
| 2. Central Bank notes | 4,368 | |
| 3. Deposits | 8,488 | |
| Securities | *1,797* | 10 |
| 4. Bonds | 1,500 | |
| 5. Stocks | 297 | |
| Insurance funds | *2,881* | 16 |
| 6. Life insurance | 31 | |
| 7. Pension fund | 960 | |
| 8. Labour old age insurance | 1,890 | |

Lines 1 and 2: Outside the banking system.
Line 3: Non-government deposits (including free deposits at the Central Bank, excluding interbank deposits).
Line 4: Total of private and government bonds registered at the Istanbul Bourse minus bonds held in bank portfolios. Only a fraction of the government debt is in the form of negotiable bonds which are listed on the Bourse.
Line 5: Principal stocks registered at the Istanbul Bourse. Balance believed to be minor.
Line 6: Actuarial reserves of the life insurance companies (figure is that of 1959 which is the last figure published).
Line 7: Total assets of the Government Employees' Pension Fund.
Line 8: Calculated as premiums collected minus benefits paid since the insurance started.

*Sources.*
*Lines 1, 2, 3, 4, 5*: Türkiye Cumhuriyet Merkez Bankası A.Ş., *Aylık Bülten*, No. 6, 1963, Ankara.

*Line 6*: İstatistik Umum Müdürlüğü, *1959, İstatistik Yıllığı*, 1961, Ankara.
*Lines 7 and 8*: State Institute of Statistics, *Monthly Bulletin of Statistics*, March 1963, Ankara.

Table 1 shows that the banking system has a very large share in the financial structure of Turkey because the assets created by the banks account for seventy-four per cent of the total shown. In fact, due to a probable over-estimate in the value of outstanding government bonds,[5] the share of the banking system may even be higher.[6]

The high share of the banking system puts financial development into a very close relation with monetary phenomena. This follows from the nature of the Central Bank and the commercial bank transactions, as is evidenced by the two sides of the consolidated balance-sheet of the system. The liabilities of the banking system have the unique characteristic of serving as the money stock. On the other side, the assets of this system constitute the source of finance for the economy. In the words of the famous Macmillan Committee Report on Finance and Industry in Great Britain in 1931:

> "The banking system thus forms the vital link between the two aspects of the complex structure with which we have to deal. For it relates the problems of the price level with the problems of finance, since the price level is undoubtedly influenced by the mass purchasing power which the banking system creates and controls, and by the structure of the credit which it builds upon the basis of available supplies of gold. Thus questions relating to the volume of purchasing power and questions relating to the distribution of purchasing power find a common focus in the banking system."[7]

In view of this property, the analysis in the following two sections will be principally an analysis of the asset and liability structure of the banking system in Turkey, and the impact of developments in this structure on the general functioning of the economy. The problems that have to do with the liabilities of the banking system—financial assets held by the non-bank public—will be the subject of the next section. The issues concerning the financial assets of the banking system—financial liabilities of the people—will be discussed in the third section, where the supply of capital funds and its allocation is considered. An attempt will be made in a framework of financial flow accounts to put the financial transfers into a perspective both with respect to the ultimate sources and uses of funds and other significant transfers.

The significance of financial policy with regard to economic development need not be one of only using the financial system to transfer and reallocate funds. Of greater importance in the long run is the dynamic aspect; the policy should also be to change the financial structure. This essentially is the problem of the development of the market and the mechanism for financial transactions in ways that will activate the wealth structure of the economy and facilitate the division of labour and specialization in the use of the productive resources of the country. Some thoughts suggested by the Turkish experience will be discussed in the last section.

## BANKING SYSTEM, MONEY AND PRICES

The financial assets supplied through the banking system—the liabilities of the banks—consist of bank notes issued by the Central Bank and deposit accounts provided by other banking institutions. Although in general terms the relation between these assets and the money supply is very close—the only obvious omission being coins which are issued by the Treasury in Turkey—a more precise definition has to take into account the peculiarities of these assets as well as the purpose of the analysis.

Table 2 shows the main categories of financial assets created by the banking system plus coins issued by the Treasury for the period 1933–62 in Turkey. The bank notes and coins are the money proper in the sense that they are the most liquid assets. But there are many *a priori* arguments concerning whether the different kinds of deposits are to be defined as money or not. The usual attitude considers as money only sight deposits upon which cheques can be drawn. The reasoning behind this attitude is that time deposits are not immediately available, and that deposits not subject to cheque can be spent only by being converted first into currency. Sometimes the additional point is made that the velocity of time deposits is lower than the velocity of sight deposits. These *a priori* arguments are by no means sufficient or conclusive. First of all, too much emphasis is put on the means-of-payment aspect of money—that is, the idea of money as something spent rather than as something held. With respect to the relation between the money stock and expenditure volume, there is no difference of kind between spending by cheque and drawing out money directly from the bank and spending it. Surely there is some difference of degree. But this difference of degree, although much less, is by no means absent in countries where payment by cheque is more common, as the existence in every bank account of many cheques payable to "cash" will indicate. Actually, this difference of degree is present even in the case of a dime and a hundred dollar bill.

TABLE 2: COINS, BANK NOTES, AND DEPOSITS, 1933–62
(In million TL)

| Year | Coins | Notes | Vault cash | "Commercial" deposits | "Saving" deposits | All deposits |
|---|---|---|---|---|---|---|
| | (1) | (2) | (3) | (4) | (5) | (6) |
| 1933 | 9 | 144 | 45 | 61 | 68 | 191 |
| 4 | 9 | 146 | 50 | 60 | 68 | 189 |
| 5 | 13 | 149 | 50 | 62 | 70 | 195 |
| 6 | 19 | 155 | 47 | 75 | 78 | 228 |
| 7 | 24 | 164 | 47 | 92 | 91 | 274 |
| 8 | 26 | 165 | 49 | 101 | 100 | 306 |
| 9 | 27 | 229 | 62 | 98 | 92 | 294 |
| 1940 | 29 | 336 | 65 | 94 | 97 | 280 |
| 1 | 30 | 477 | 57 | 117 | 107 | 345 |
| 2 | 31 | 605 | 64 | 159 | 130 | 438 |
| 3 | 32 | 732 | 74 | 169 | 137 | 468 |
| 4 | 32 | 907 | 74 | 170 | 168 | 509 |
| 5 | 36 | 944 | 71 | 190 | 226 | 567 |
| 6 | 38 | 877 | 74 | 214 | 274 | 657 |
| 7 | 36 | 946 | 77 | 229 | 365 | 781 |
| 8 | 62 | 899 | 83 | 256 | 407 | 913 |
| 9 | 70 | 909 | 93 | 254 | 470 | 993 |
| 1950 | 63 | 921 | 97 | 251 | 524 | 1,065 |
| 1 | 43 | 1,034 | 123 | 332 | 662 | 1,416 |
| 2 | 44 | 1,190 | 147 | 438 | 817 | 1,897 |
| 3 | 49 | 1,337 | 169 | 583 | 1,027 | 2,486 |
| 4 | 53 | 1,487 | 198 | 730 | 1,295 | 3,004 |
| 5 | 59 | 1,764 | 238 | 878 | 1,576 | 3,481 |
| 6 | 66 | 2,185 | 282 | 1,029 | 2,001 | 4,250 |
| 7 | 77 | 2,900 | 333 | 1,153 | 2,684 | 5,262 |
| 8 | 90 | 3,526 | 440 | 1,291 | 3,228 | 6,054 |
| 9 | 104 | 3,600 | 557 | 1,498 | 3,701 | 6,977 |
| 1960 | 124 | 4,195 | 678 | 1,655 | 4,203 | 7,912 |
| 1 | 150 | 4,581 | 788 | 1,746 | 4,651 | 8,375 |
| 2 | 189 | 4,911 | 808 | 1,853 | 5,218 | 9,136 |

*Coins:* Quantity issued, which includes coin lying in vaults of Central and commercial banks.
*Notes:* Bank note liability of the Central Bank.
*Vault cash:* Notes and coin in vaults of commercial banks and coins in Central Bank.
"*Commercial*" *deposits:* For 1933–43, estimated by deducting official deposits and interbank deposits from a classification titled "other deposits". For 1944–49, merchants' deposits. For 1950–62, commercial deposits.
"*Saving*" *deposits:* As defined in text.
*All deposits:* Col. 4 and col. 5 and blocked commercial deposits and official deposits.
*Dating:* In order to estimate an average value for each item over the calendar year, the data were processed as follows: For coins, averages of monthly figures (1933–52) and averages of beginning and end-of-year figures (1953–62). For notes,

averages of weekly figures. For vault cash and deposits of all types, averages of beginning and end-of-year figures.
*Source:* Compiled from Central Bank *Monthly Bulletins.*

As to the other argument, there is no reason why all components of the money stock must have the same velocity. The fact that goods on the lower counters of a store have a high turnover does not mean that the goods of the same kind on the upper shelves are not part of the desired inventory. Particularly in underdeveloped countries, there probably is currency of very low velocity hidden in chests or pillows which is nevertheless considered part of the money stock. Why should deposits of the same nature not be?

A more functional approach to the definition of money is to identify the categories of assets the volume of which shows a stable relationship with the phenomenon we want to explain—in this case, changes in the price level. Three practical tests can be applied. First, if an asset has a high degree of "moneyness", then it should be expected to have a high rate of substitution with money proper, namely currency. The trend of the deposit-currency ratios over time may give an idea about this aspect. Secondly, if an asset is *not* money, if it is not held for the convenience it yields as ready purchasing power, then there should be some other reason for holding it. And thirdly, if an asset *is* held mainly for the purpose of providing ready purchasing power, a money definition including this asset would be expected to give a better explanation of changes in the price level than a money definition excluding this asset.

In Turkey, deposits are classified as commercial deposits, saving deposits, official deposits, and interbank deposits. Each of these can be either sight deposits or time deposits. Commercial deposits are those of private legal entities: firms, partnerships, corporations, and similar organizations. The saving deposits are those of individuals.[8] According to this classification, if somebody has a grocery store and he deposits money as the owner or manager of this store, this will be a "commercial deposit". But if he deposits the same money as an individual, this will be a "saving deposit". Official deposits are those of the government departments and state organizations. The fourth category, interbank deposits, has the usual meaning. Nothing in the banking law or the commercial code forbids the banks to grant checking rights for all these deposits, but in practice the banks do not do so for "saving deposits", with very rare exceptions.

The deposits held by the non-bank public are the "commercial deposits" and the "saving deposits". We are not interested here in interbank deposits, which cancel out when we consolidate the balance sheets of the banking system, and we are not interested in official deposits, which belong to the government rather than to the non-bank public.

Although both the "saving" and the "commercial" deposits have a time deposit component, the distinction in practice seems to be less important, as arrangements are easily made to draw time deposits before their due dates. In the case of commercial deposits, however, there is a portion which has accrued as import prepayments and which is "blocked". The Central Bank Bulletin gives figures for a sub-category of "commercial deposits" which is "either blocked or time deposits". As it was impossible at the moment to find out what proportion of these time commercial deposits was not blocked, and as the total amount was small, this sub-category was not included in our "commercial deposit" figures.

As far as "commercial deposits" are concerned, it seems clear that at interest rates around two per cent when prices were rising by ten to twenty per cent per annum, people could not have held these deposits solely as income-producing investments. The same thing applies to the sight component of "saving deposits". Even time deposits have never yielded more than 6·5 per cent per annum since 1933. Therefore it seems plausible to assume that deposits in Turkey are held more for their moneyness than as investments for a pecuniary return.

In the framework of the quantity theory, the demand for money depends in general on the price level and real income. The higher prices are, the more money people will hold. In this relationship between the money stock and the price level, real balances (money/price level) will tend to rise as real income rises. It has been observed in many empirical studies that this is not a 1 : 1 relationship between the real balances and the real income. When real income grows, the demand for real balances increases more than proportionately. In other words, the income elasticity of the demand for money is greater than 1; money is a "luxury good". In the following paragraphs the relationship between increases in monetary assets, the general price level, and real income during the years from 1933 to 1962 will be analysed.

The Central Bank of Turkey was established in 1931, and by 1933 had started to play its role as a bank of issue. In the course of the three decades after 1933, the price level multiplied about twelvefold, and the money supply as defined below multiplied some forty-sevenfold. Most of the price increases occurred in two distinct inflationary periods (Diagram 1). These were the Second World War years and

DIAGRAM 1: CURRENCY, DEPOSITS, AND PRICES

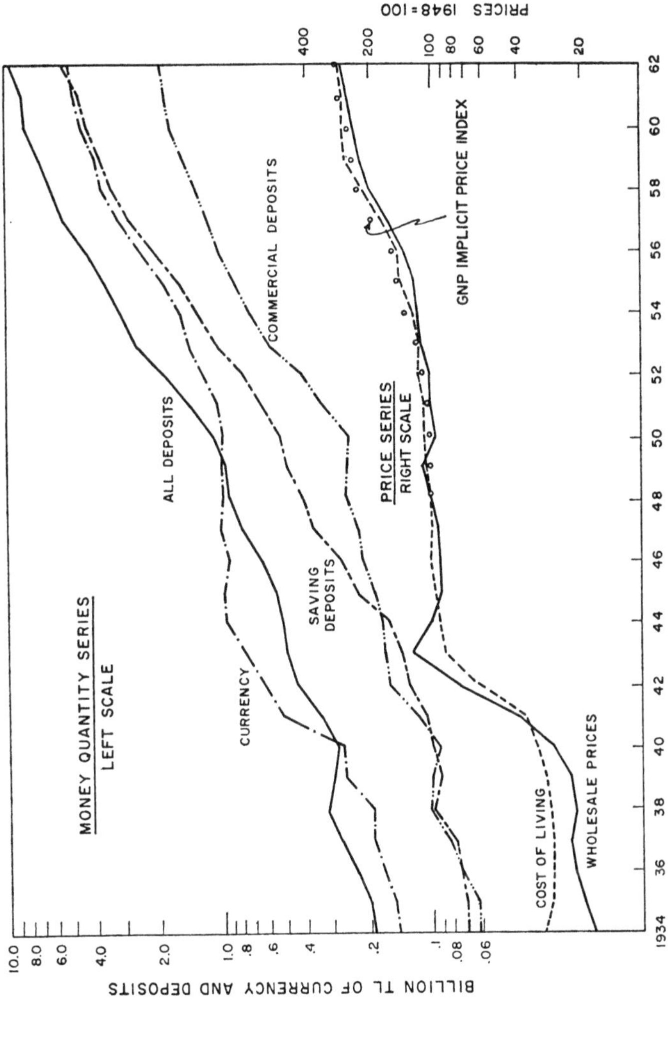


*Sources:* Tables 2 and 3. Currency is coins plus notes.

the years of inflationary development strategy after 1950. In the first case, from 1939 to 1943, the price increases averaged about forty per cent per annum, with a slower rate of increase (twenty-five per cent) in the first half and a higher rate of increase (seventy per cent) in the second half. This inflation followed a period of stable prices from 1933 to 1939 and came to an abrupt end in 1944, with a slight fall in the level of prices.

TABLE 3: PRICE INDICES, 1933–62
(1948 = 100)

| Year | *Wholesale prices* | *Cost of living* | *Average of 1 and 2* | *GNP implicit price index* |
|---|---|---|---|---|
| | (1) | (2) | (3) | (4) |
| 1933 | 17 | 31 | 24 | |
| 4 | 17 | 30 | 24 | |
| 5 | 19 | 27 | 23 | |
| 6 | 21 | 27 | 24 | |
| 7 | 22 | 27 | 24 | |
| 8 | 21 | 28 | 24 | |
| 9 | 22 | 29 | 25 | |
| 1940 | 27 | 32 | 29 | |
| 1 | 38 | 37 | 37 | |
| 2 | 73 | 62 | 67 | |
| 3 | 127 | 86 | 106 | |
| 4 | 98 | 92 | 95 | |
| 5 | 95 | 97 | 96 | |
| 6 | 92 | 102 | 97 | |
| 7 | 93 | 95 | 94 | |
| 8 | 100 | 100 | 100 | 100 |
| 9 | 108 | 106 | 107 | 103 |
| 1950 | 97 | 103 | 100 | 99 |
| 1 | 103 | 106 | 104 | 102 |
| 2 | 104 | 111 | 107 | 109 |
| 3 | 107 | 114 | 110 | 116 |
| 4 | 118 | 123 | 120 | 130 |
| 5 | 127 | 145 | 136 | 143 |
| 6 | 148 | 156 | 152 | 161 |
| 7 | 175 | 180 | 177 | 193 |
| 8 | 202 | 214 | 208 | 216 |
| 9 | 242 | 266 | 254 | 256 |
| 1960 | 255 | 273 | 264 | 266 |
| 1 | 262 | 272 | 267 | 281 |
| 2 | 277 | 280 | 278 | 286 |

*Sources:* Wholesale prices for 1933–37 from Istanbul Chamber of Commerce, and for 1938–62 from Ministry of Commerce. Cost of living is for Ankara, from State Institute of Statistics. The implicit GNP deflator is from the State Institute of Statistics, except the last two years which were spliced using the wholesale price index. All data compiled from *Monthly Bulletin of Statistics.*

After a period of stable prices following the Second World War, prices started to rise again after 1950. This time the beginning and the end of the rapid inflation were dissimilar to the earlier case: prices started rising slowly at about five per cent per annum from 1950 to 1953, then inflation gained momentum averaging fifteen per cent per annum from 1953 to 1959, followed by another period of about five per cent per annum price increase.

Without going into the refinements of theory and statistics, Diagram 1 suggests a close relation between money and prices. Whenever prices were rising rapidly, the rate of increase in the money categories was also high. Whenever the increase in the money categories slowed, the prices also slowed or stopped rising. The degree of coincidence of the turning points was also high.

This crude observation about the relationship between money and prices in an underdeveloped country such as Turkey can be supported by *a priori* arguments as well. No matter how much validity can be attributed to the Keynesian criticism of the quantity theory analysis for the developed economies—the recent endorsement of it in the Radcliffe Report in Britain considers money the "small change" of the total liquidity—it would be difficult to justify the neglect of the stock of money as *the* most important factor affecting the volume of expenditures in a country where financial development is in its infancy. Particularly in a country such as Turkey, where money seems to be the only significant financial asset, it would be difficult to defend the view that "money does not matter".

However, the actual test of the hypothesis has to be empirical. To attempt such an empirical verification, we must make precise the quantitative magnitudes—that is, define the price level and the money stock.

Several price indices are available, some of them for the entire period we are considering, others for more recent years. These are shown in Diagram 1. The fact that for the long period considered they move close together simplifies the task of choice. The only important divergence between the cost of living and wholesale price indices arises when pre- and post-war years are compared. This could be due mainly to the divergence between bread and wheat prices, which was caused by a government policy of price supports for wheat and subsidies for bread, as well as to rent controls. For our purposes, neither the prices at which there is no market (goods not available) nor the prices which would have prevailed if there were no controls are relevant. For this reason a compromise was believed to be as good as any analysis, and an arithmetic average of the two series was used for the period during which we must depend on wholesale or cost of living indices. For the period from 1948 to 1960 we have an additional price series: the implicit price index of GNP, which was used for this period. Price controls and black market operations have distorted the price indices. However, over long periods these prices were probably adjusted, thus relieving the general trend from these biases.

The sums that could be considered money are the following: coins and bank notes, commercial deposits, and "saving deposits". The *a priori* arguments for and against including deposits in the money supply were discussed above. Here we shall examine the plausible alternative definitions of money to see which best explains the trend of prices relative to the changes in real income. These alternative money definitions are:

1. Currency, which is coins+bank notes issued;
2. Currency outside the banks+non-blocked "commercial sight deposits";
3. Second definition+"saving deposits";
4. Third definition+blocked "commercial deposits" and official deposits.

According to these definitions of money stock, four income velocities are calculated (Diagram 2). As can be seen, the third and the fourth velocities, which are computed with money definitions that include "saving" and all deposits respectively, are more stable than the first and second velocities, which exclude "saving" and total deposits. Not only are the first two velocities less stable, but their trend is upward over time, which is contrary to normal expectations. It has been observed that when real income rises the income velocity of money usually falls. Monetization is probably still going on in Turkey, which would be an additional reason for a falling trend in velocity.

In order to make a more quantitative check, a correlation analysis was made. The velocity using definition 1 was so obviously unstable that it was not bothered about. A simple correlation was run between real balances, computed according to each of the last three definitions, and real income. In order to relate the rates of change in these series, rather than the actual magnitudes to each other, the variables were taken in log values. In this way the b coefficient of the regression equation gives us the elasticity of the demand for real balances with respect to real income.

The results of these correlations were as follows:

$$\frac{\text{Money 2}}{\text{Price Level}} \text{ on Real Income}$$

$$r = 0{\cdot}9056$$
$$b = 0{\cdot}82$$

$$\frac{\text{Money 3}}{\text{Price Level}} \text{ on Real Income}$$

$$r = 0{\cdot}9576$$
$$b = 1{\cdot}176$$

$$\frac{\text{Money 4}}{\text{Price Level}} \text{ on Real Income}$$

$$r = 0{\cdot}9533$$
$$b = 1{\cdot}2000$$

As in most economic time series, the correlation coefficient is not very significant due to the serial correlation involved and the interdependence of observations. Even then, a comparison of the correlation coefficients lends weight to the hypothesis that a money stock including the "saving deposits" (Money 3 or 4) explains the trend in the price level better than a definition of money which excludes "saving deposits" (Money 2). As between Money 3 and 4, we choose 3 on *a priori* grounds. The theoretical values for prices computed from Money 3 are compared in Diagram 3 with actual price changes in Turkey during the thirty years. The closeness of the theoretical and actual values for price indices cannot be entirely attributed to the trend factor.

To summarize, in the thirty years from 1933 to 1962, the money supply (which includes a very high proportion of the existing financial assets in Turkey) increased by 13·7 per cent per annum on the average. This increase can be divided into three parts: 9·5 per cent corresponding with the increase in prices, 3·8 per cent corresponding with the increase in real income, and 0·4 per cent corresponding with the fall in velocity.

This analysis also shows that if this trend continues it may be possible to increase the money supply in Turkey by 0·18 times more than the real growth rate without causing inflation. This means that if the Five Year Plan's target of seven per cent growth in real income is achieved, the money supply may increase by about 8·3 per cent per annum without creating inflation. This corresponds to about 1·7 per cent of the GNP and about ten per cent of the gross investment that has been planned.

DIAGRAM 2: INCOME VELOCITIES OF MONEY ACCORDING TO FOUR DEFINITIONS OF MONEY

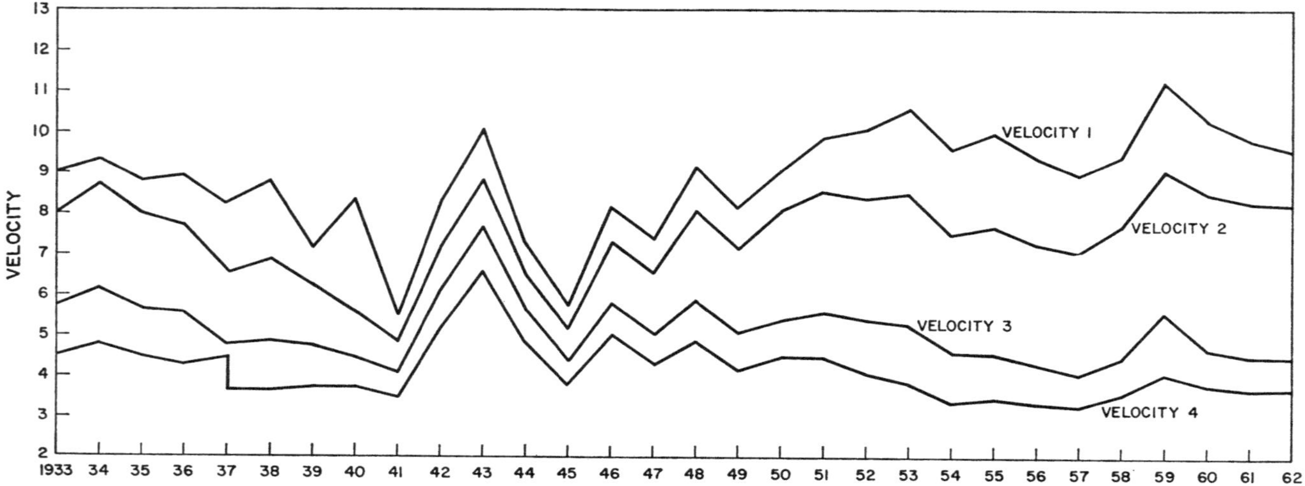


*Source:* Calculated from Table 4.

TABLE 4: MONEY SUPPLY, REAL INCOME AND PRICES, 1933–62

| *Year* | *Money 1* | *Money 2* | *Money 3* | *Money 4* | *Prices* | *Real income* |
|---|---|---|---|---|---|---|
| | (in million TL) | | | | 1948 = 100 | 1948 Prices |
| 1933 | 153 | 169 | 237 | 299 | 24 | 5,728 |
| 4 | 155 | 165 | 233 | 294 | 24 | 5,988 |
| 5 | 162 | 174 | 244 | 307 | 23 | 6,111 |
| 6 | 174 | 202 | 280 | 355 | 24 | 6,483 |
| 7 | 188 | 233 | 324 | 415 | 24 | 6,497 |
| 8 | 191 | 243 | 343 | 448 | 24 | 7,038 |
| 9 | 256 | 292 | 384 | 488 | 25 | 7,420 |
| 1940 | 265 | 394 | 491 | 580 | 29 | 7,690 |
| 1 | 507 | 567 | 674 | 795 | 37 | 7,528 |
| 2 | 636 | 731 | 861 | 1,010 | 67 | 7,888 |
| 3 | 764 | 859 | 996 | 1,158 | 106 | 7,251 |
| 4 | 939 | 1,032 | 1,200 | 1,374 | 95 | 7,166 |
| 5 | 980 | 1,081 | 1,307 | 1,476 | 96 | 5,942 |
| 6 | 915 | 1,020 | 1,294 | 1,498 | 97 | 7,755 |
| 7 | 982 | 1,091 | 1,456 | 1,686 | 94 | 7,748 |
| 8 | 961 | 1,082 | 1,489 | 1,791 | 100 | 8,815 |
| 9 | 979 | 1,097 | 1,567 | 1,879 | 103 | 7,828 |
| 1950 | 984 | 1,104 | 1,628 | 1,952 | 99 | 9,098 |
| 1 | 1,077 | 1,229 | 1,891 | 2,370 | 102 | 10,496 |
| 2 | 1,234 | 1,474 | 2,290 | 2,984 | 109 | 11,393 |
| 3 | 1,386 | 1,723 | 2,750 | 3,703 | 116 | 12,665 |
| 4 | 1,540 | 1,953 | 3,248 | 4,341 | 130 | 11,461 |
| 5 | 1,823 | 2,340 | 3,916 | 5,066 | 143 | 12,334 |
| 6 | 2,251 | 2,883 | 4,884 | 6,219 | 161 | 13,169 |
| 7 | 2,977 | 3,704 | 6,388 | 7,906 | 193 | 13,989 |
| 8 | 3,616 | 4,380 | 7,608 | 9,230 | 216 | 15,664 |
| 9 | 3,704 | 4,550 | 8,251 | 10,124 | 256 | 16,312 |
| 1960 | 4,319 | 5,192 | 9,395 | 11,553 | 266 | 16,677 |
| 1 | 4,731 | 5,575 | 10,226 | 12,318 | 381 | 16,551 |
| 2 | 5,100 | 6,009 | 11,227 | 13,428 | 286 | 17,577 |

*Definitions*: Money 1 is coins+bank notes issued. Money 2 is coins+bank notes−vault cash+"commercial deposits". Money 3 is coins+bank notes−vault cash+"commercial deposits"+"saving" deposits. Money 4 is coins+bank notes—vault cash + all deposits. Prices for 1933-47 are an average of the wholesale price index and the cost of living index, and for 1948–62 are the GNP implicit price index. Real income for 1933–47 is as estimated by Aysel Yenal, and for 1948–62 as given by the State Institute of Statistics.
*Source:* Tables 2 and 3; Aysel Yenal, Doçent's thesis, Istanbul, 1963; and State Institute of Statistics.

The determinants of the money supply can be analysed at different levels. In the first instance, it can be said that bank notes and coins are supplied in amounts according to the policy of the Central Bank and the Treasury respectively, and that the outstanding balance of deposit accounts is the result of decisions by individuals who want to keep some proportion of their assets at the banks. Going one step beyond, if a stable and regular relationship can be assumed between

DIAGRAM 3: ACTUAL PRICES COMPARED WITH THEORETICAL PRICES

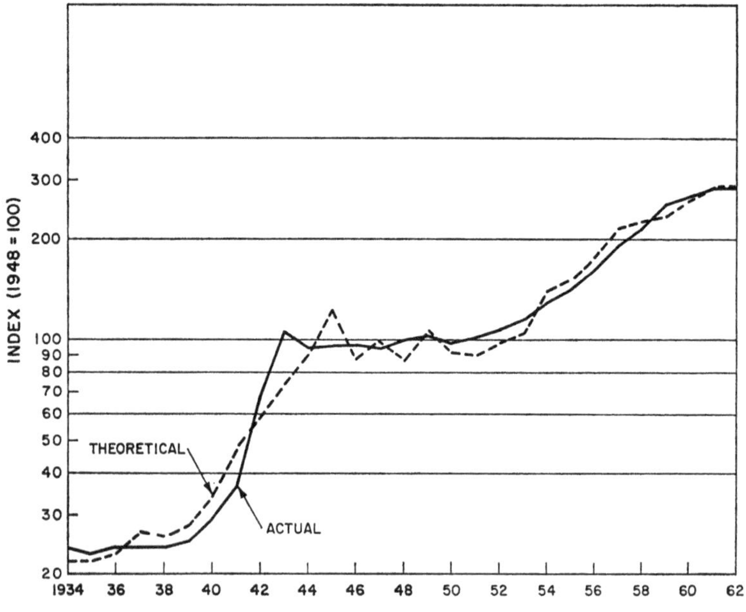


*Sources:* Table 3 and Regression Equation 3.

deposits and currency outside the banks, and if the currency held by the banks is expressed as a ratio of total deposits, then a supply function for monetary assets can be written as follows:[9]

$$M = C + D = B \frac{\frac{D}{R}\left(1+\frac{D}{C}\right)}{\frac{D}{R} + \frac{D}{C}}$$

where

M: total money stock
D: monetary deposits
B: bank notes+coins = currency
R: bank reserves
C: currency outside banks = B−R

In this formula the total money stock is expressed as a function of (*a*) bank note and coin supply, (*b*) deposit-currency ratio, and (*c*) deposit-reserve ratio. These variables correspond to the behaviour of each of the following parties respectively: (*a*) the Central Bank (and the Treasury for coins), which determines the currency supply; (*b*) individuals, who determine what proportions of their desired money balances to keep in the banks rather than in their pockets; and (*c*) the banks, which determine what proportion of the currency entrusted to them to transfer into the hands of the public and which the recipients will again divide between the banks and their pockets.

In Turkey, coins are issued by the Treasury subject to the maximum limits specified by law. Bank notes are issued by the Central Bank against assets such as gold, foreign exchange, government bills, and commercial paper. There are no limits to the total of bank notes that can be issued, or even to the volume of bank notes that can be issued with fiduciary backing.[10] In spite of the complicated rules with respect to the amounts of notes that can be issued for different kinds of assets, and in spite of the semi-independent character of the Bank's management in theory,[11] it was in practice as if the government had almost unlimited authority to determine the amount it wanted to borrow from the Central Bank and thus to influence the amount of paper money in circulation. This does not mean that all changes in the bank note supply have been initiated by the government. Changes in foreign exchange, gold stocks, and some other minor accounts (e.g. rediscounts of the bills of the private sector) have also affected the monetary liabilities of the Central Bank;[12] however, as is shown in Diagram 4, by far the most important determinant of the bank note supply has been borrowing by the state sector. In fact, at the end of 1962, as against a bank note issue amounting to 5,077 million Turkish liras, the total of the net loans to the state sector (loans to the government budget and the state economic enterprises minus official deposits) was 5,291 million liras.

Foreign transactions had a slight dampening effect on the bank note increase in the first three years of the Second World War. Thereafter, due to the difficulties of importing goods during the worst years of the war, and also to the heavy demands for Turkish exports by the warring countries, Turkey had surpluses in foreign trade and accumulated gold reserves which had a slightly expansionist effect on the bank note supply. This pattern lasted until 1947. After that, continuous foreign trade deficits enabled the government to borrow a little more than the increase in note supply. In 1946 and 1960, the years when the Turkish lira was officially devalued, there was a rise in the value of net foreign assets (in terms of Turkish lira) held by the Bank. This gain was used to write off some of the government's debt to the Central Bank which explains the compensating fluctuations on those two dates in the diagram.

TABLE 5 : DETERMINANTS OF CENTRAL BANK NOTE ISSUE, 1933–62

(End of year data in million TL)

| *Year* | *State sector* | + | *Private sector* | + | *Foreign sector* | + | *Undistributable* | = | *Notes in circulation* |
|---|---|---|---|---|---|---|---|---|---|
| 1933 | 2 | | −12 | | 17 | | 140 | | 147 |
| 4 | 7 | | −14 | | 17 | | 148 | | 158 |
| 5 | 4 | | −26 | | 17 | | 169 | | 164 |
| 6 | 21 | | 8 | | 44 | | 98 | | 171 |
| 7 | 41 | | 9 | | 34 | | 81 | | 165 |
| 8 | 84 | | 0 | | 19 | | 86 | | 189 |
| 9 | 208 | | −7 | | 1 | | 80 | | 282 |
| 1940 | 331 | | −21 | | 29 | | 64 | | 403 |
| 1 | 415 | | −11 | | 74 | | 35 | | 513 |
| 2 | 605 | | 28 | | 103 | | −3 | | 734 |
| 3 | 580 | | 45 | | 196 | | −9 | | 802 |
| 4 | 704 | | 50 | | 218 | | −11 | | 961 |
| 5 | 612 | | 72 | | 240 | | −43 | | 881 |
| 6 | 635 | | 91 | | 548 | | −337 | | 937 |
| 7 | 384 | | 88 | | 469 | | −52 | | 889 |
| 8 | 628 | | 42 | | 320 | | −58 | | 932 |
| 9 | 611 | | 83 | | 259 | | −60 | | 893 |
| 1950 | 931 | | 73 | | 18 | | −60 | | 962 |
| 1 | 1,142 | | 108 | | 36 | | −140 | | 1,146 |
| 2 | 1,298 | | 354 | | −207 | | −194 | | 1,251 |
| 3 | 1,526 | | 249 | | 8 | | −315 | | 1,468 |
| 4 | 1,899 | | 340 | | −167 | | −539 | | 1,533 |
| 5 | 2,624 | | 231 | | −416 | | −431 | | 2,008 |
| 6 | 3,083 | | 147 | | −293 | | −386 | | 2,551 |
| 7 | 3,894 | | 483 | | −585 | | −572 | | 3,220 |
| 8 | 4,264 | | 570 | | −405 | | −956 | | 3,473 |
| 9 | 4,655 | | 814 | | −874 | | −704 | | 3,891 |
| 1960 | 4,633 | | 702 | | −357 | | −526 | | 4,452 |
| 1 | 4,800 | | 478 | | −380 | | −115 | | 4,783 |
| 2 | 5,291 | | 460 | | −528 | | −101 | | 5,127 |

*Explanation:* Notes in circulation are a liability of the Central Bank. The table is constructed by assigning all the other asset and liability accounts of the Central Bank to one of the three sectors, or to the undistributable column when the correct sector could not be clearly identified. Positive figures indicate that the Central Bank had a net claim on the sector; negative figures indicate a net liability to the sector. The balance sheet accounts of the Central Bank were distributed as follows:

*State sector:* Credits to finance central and annexed budgets plus credits to state economic enterprises minus official deposits.

*Private sector:* Credits to private businesses, including to agricultural borrowers, minus private deposits.

*Foreign sector:* Gold and foreign exchange assets minus gold and foreign exchange liabilities minus counterpart deposits.

*Sources:* Compiled from Central Bank *Monthly Bulletins.*

DIAGRAM 4: SELECTED DETERMINANTS OF CHANGE IN NOTE SUPPLY

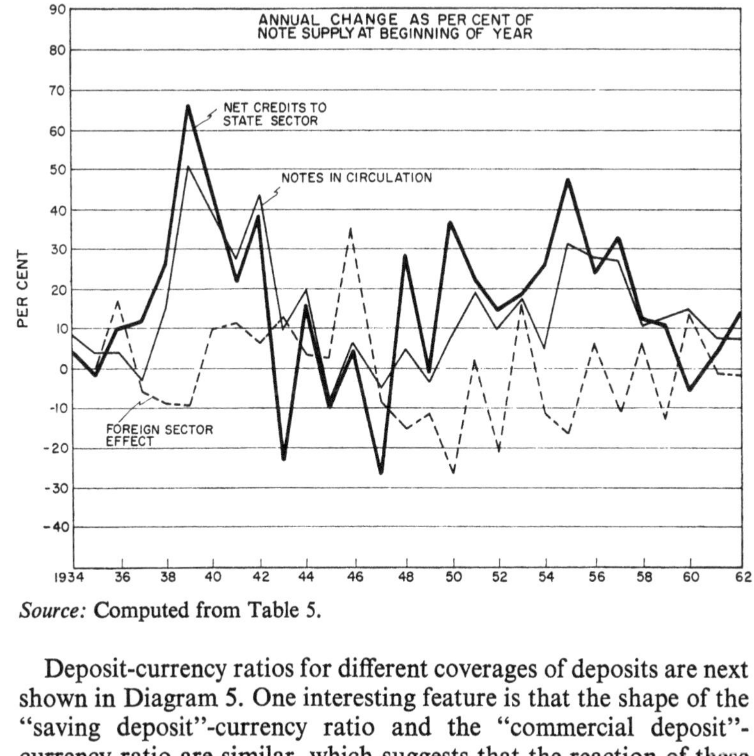


*Source:* Computed from Table 5.

Deposit-currency ratios for different coverages of deposits are next shown in Diagram 5. One interesting feature is that the shape of the "saving deposit"-currency ratio and the "commercial deposit"-currency ratio are similar, which suggests that the reaction of these deposits to changes in the quantity of currency is similar. Thus, from the standpoint of moneyness, "saving deposits" are like "commercial deposits".[13]

The pattern of changes in deposit-currency ratios can be easily explained. There is a big fall during the Second World War years. It would be very strange if this did not happen. Although Turkey never entered the war, it suffered all the difficulties and anxieties of the war years, and there even were one or two runs on the banks. People were moving to the countryside from the big population centres, or they were preparing themselves to move. This atmosphere was enough to account for the preference of people to hold their money in the form of currency rather than deposits. Some people

DIAGRAM 5: DEPOSIT RATIOS

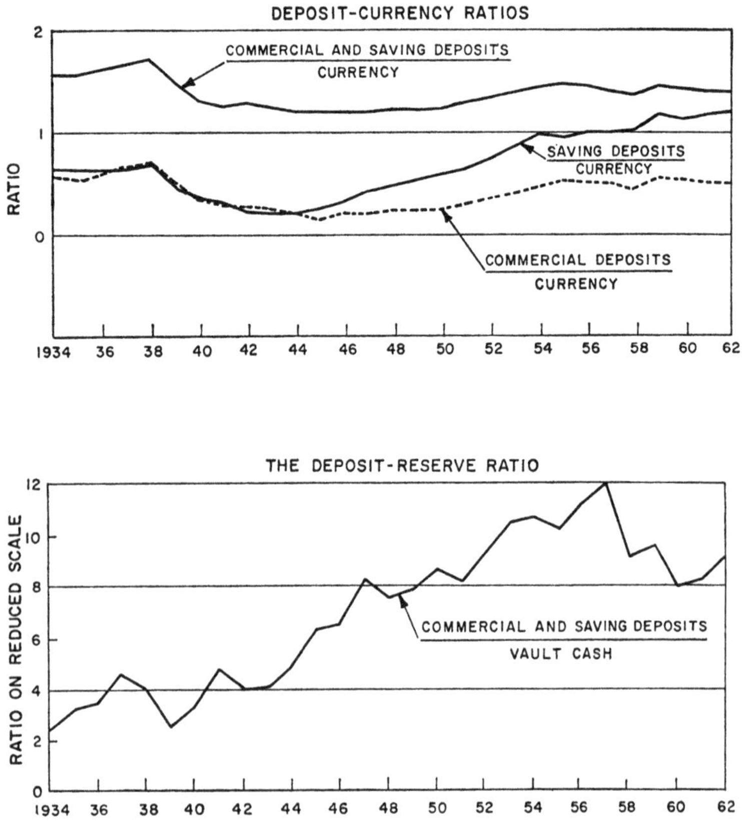


*Source:* Table 2. Currency is coins plus notes minus vault cash.

actually preferred to have it in gold coins, which resulted in rapid rises in the price of gold.

In the post-war years the deposit-currency ratio not only attained its pre-war level, but showed a steady rise beyond this level until 1954. This was probably due to the very rapid development of commercial banking at that time. After 1954, this tendency seems to have diminished or stopped. From 1954 to 1962 the ratio of the sum of commercial and "saving" deposits to currency remains relatively stable at around 1·5.

The third factor to consider is the deposit-reserve ratio. Reserve here means *only* the currency held by commercial banks (leakage of currency from the public back into the banking system). All the other reserves are not relevant to our present inquiry because we are interested in the way banks decide between holding in their vaults the currency they receive as deposits or giving it out as credits.[14] The banks may withhold or return currency to the public and thus affect the quantity of currency which is in the hands of the public—that quantity being the denominator of the deposit-currency ratio. The important question is, how much currency do they keep in their vaults as compared to outstanding deposits, which is what we call the deposit-reserve ratio?

The trend of the deposit-reserve ratio in Turkey during the period in which we are interested is shown in Diagram 5. It starts from around 3·0 in 1933, rises to 12·0 in 1957, then falls to 9·0 in 1958, and fluctuates around this figure thereafter. Here again, the development of banking is the main factor in explaining the secular trend. As banks have established more branches and accumulated larger numbers of depositors, they have been able to manage their transactions with less vault cash. The high demand for credit has also induced the banks to keep minimum balances idle. The upward trend possibly reaches its maximum limit by 1957. The sharp fall in 1958 is due to credit ceilings that were imposed on banks as part of a stabilization programme. Ratios for 1960, 1961, and 1962 show that probably the deposit-reserve ratio has settled at about the 9 to 1 level.

Thus, we have tried to account for the supply of financial assets. In very simple terms the amount of coins has been determined by the Treasury, subject to a maximum fixed by law, the stock of bank notes in circulation has been determined mainly by the volume of government borrowing from the Central Bank, and the volume of deposits has been determined by the interaction of the following factors: the currency supply (notes and coins), the deposit-currency ratio, and the deposit-reserve ratio.

In the money-supply equation, all three determinants, namely B, $\frac{D}{C}$, and $\frac{D}{R}$, are positively related to M. During the inflation of the Second World War, when B was rising very rapidly, the $\frac{D}{C}$ ratio fell, thus dampening the increase in M. After 1944, both $\frac{D}{C}$ and $\frac{D}{R}$ rose and contributed to the increase in the money stock .The rapid increase in B, which came after 1950, was thus supplemented by rising values of both ratios to produce a very rapid increase in M. Had the ratios remained the same during the 1950s, the money supply would have risen less rapidly.

The part of the 1958 stabilization programme which imposed ceilings on bank credits forced the banks to increase their reserves and in this way diminished the $\frac{D}{R}$ ratio (see Diagram 5). The effect on the money supply of a policy measure that changes the $\frac{D}{R}$ ratio can be calculated with the help of the formula above. In the case of the 1958 measures, this effect was not very significant and definitely not worth the havoc caused by the rigid measures.

Since 1954 the $\frac{D}{C}$ and $\frac{D}{R}$ ratios have fluctuated around 1·6 and 10, respectively. If they remain stable around these values, we can say that each additional lira issued in bank notes or coins will lead to the creation of about 1·38 lira in deposits and 2·24 lira in the total money supply.

## Financial Transactions and the Allocation of Funds

In the previous section, developments in the Turkish economy connected with the liability side of the consolidated balance sheets of the banking system as a whole (including the Central Bank) were analysed to bring out the mechanism by which financial assets of the kinds existing in Turkey are accumulated and to reveal the connection between this accumulation of assets and the price level. In this section we turn our attention to the other side of the balance sheets, to consider another aspect of the same transactions: the allocation of funds.

The credit structure of the economy could be studied by analysing the assets of the banking system in isolation. But more interesting from the standpoint of economic analysis and more illuminating for economic strategy would be to link these financial transfers with the ultimate sources and uses of real resources in the economy, on the one hand, and with the non-financial transfers that can be accounted for, on the other hand. Such analysis would put into perspective the significance (or the insignificance) of financial transactions as factors in resource allocation in the economy. We have attempted this for Turkey using a very crude financial accounts system. Lack of data precludes, at least for the time being, the extension of this analysis to periods earlier than 1950 and later than 1960. However, this loss of a long-term perspective is, I believe, compensated for by the fact that the decade from 1950 to 1960 was a very interesting period in Turkish economic development. Particularly with respect to the use of monetary policies for accumulating capital, it provides almost a laboratory case: A large-scale attempt to finance development expenditures through inflationary finance had both its beginning and—it is hoped—its end within this decade.

The financial accounts for each year from 1950 to 1960 and the definitions and sources are given in the Appendix. It should be recognized that these tables are necessarily crude. Many problems of identification and classification are still unresolved, as the categories for "undistributable" and "errors and omissions" indicate. The notes show that some assumptions had to be made in order to fit the available figures into the financial accounts framework. But at the level of generality of the analysis based on them, these defects will not be significant. The general format of these tables is also shown in a summary table for the whole period which follows as Table 6.

Before we pass to an analysis of the allocation of funds which has been effected through monetary transfers, a brief explanation of the kinds of institutions and the types of transactions which they have may be useful. The asset portfolio of the Central Bank is classified both according to the type of paper and according to the debtors' sectors. One difficulty is that from neither of these two classifications is it possible to separate the credits that are granted through the intermediary of another bank from those given directly. This had to be deduced from an examination of the balance sheets of the banks. At the end of 1960 the distribution of loans by the Central Bank was as follows:

| | *Million TL* | *Per cent* |
|---|---|---|
| To central government | 1,427 | 22·3 |
| state enterprises | 3,811 | 59·6 |
| agriculture | 329 | 5·1 |
| business | 822 | 12·9 |
| Total | 6,389 | 100·0 |

Regardless of their nature or classification, most of the loans to public bodies had become long-term or even non-redeemable loans. In fact, in 1961, a consolidation act converted almost all the Bank's loans to public bodies into treasury bonds carrying interest of 0·5 per cent and repayable in six-monthly instalments over one hundred years.

The state banks, sometimes referred to as banks established by special laws, are essentially holding companies or investment banks, with one possible exception. The most important are the Sümerbank (the largest state organization which owns plants in textiles, cement, paper, wood processing, metal pipes, and in many other fields), Etibank (responsible for exploiting mines and hydraulic energy), Maritime Bank (running passenger and freight lines on domestic and foreign shipping routes), and Building and Credit Bank (the only mortgage bank for housing). The exception is the Agricultural Bank, which, although it participates significantly in industry, is essentially a commercial bank. Except for this one, the resources of the state banks characteristically are largely from their own capital or obtained by credits from the Central Bank, and their assets are either fixed assets or long-term credits.

At the end of 1959, the sources of funds of these state banks, expressed as percentages of their total sources, were: from their own capital, thirty-nine per cent; from loans by the Central Bank, twenty-seven per cent; and from deposits, twenty-seven per cent. They had utilized these funds in the following manner: for investments in state enterprises (usually their own subsidiaries), forty-five per cent; and credit to agriculture, thirty-three per cent.

The commercial banks are those banks which come under the general banking act and form a homogeneous group whose resources are mainly deposits and whose assets are the short-term commercial credits which they grant. By this criterion, the Agricultural Bank should also be classified a commercial bank. The remaining banks

TABLE 6: RESOURCES, TRANSFERS AND EXPENDITURES
1950–60
(Billion current TL)

| | *House-hold* | *Busi-ness* | *Cen-tral Govt.* | *Local Govt.* | *State Eco-nomic Enter.* | *Rest of World* | *Banks* | *Un-dis-tribu-table* |
|---|---|---|---|---|---|---|---|---|
| 1. Resources | | | | | | | | |
| 1.1. GDP | 285·2 | | | | | | | |
| 1.2. Import surplus | | | | | | 6·1 | | |
| TOTAL RESOURCES | 285·2 | | | | | 6·1 | | |
| 2. Fiscal Transfers | | | | | | | | |
| 2.1. Taxes | −33·1 | −2·3 | 31·4 | 6·1 | −2·0 | | | |
| 2.2. Other Revenue | −5·7 | | 8·9 | | | −3·2 | | |
| 2.3. Budget Transfers | 2·7 | | −4·9 | 0·6 | 0·9 | 0·6 | | |
| TOTAL FISCAL TRANS. | −36·1 | −2·3 | 35·4 | 6·7 | −1·1 | −2·6 | | |
| 3. Monetary Transfers | | | | | | | | |
| 3.1. Central Bank | −2·9 | | 1·5 | | 1·8 | −1·1 | 1·0 | −0·2 |
| 3.2. State Banks | 1·1 | 0·8 | −0·7 | 0·8 | 2·8 | | −3·2 | −1·6 |
| 3.3. Comm. Banks | −2·4 | 1·6 | 0·1 | | 0·4 | −0·1 | 1·3 | −0·8 |
| 3.4. Other Inst. | −0·4 | −0·4 | −0·8 | | −0·4 | | 1·0 | 1·0 |
| TOTAL MONETARY TRANSFERS | −4·6 | 2·0 | 0·1 | 0·8 | 4·5 | −1·2 | 0 | −1·6 |
| 4. Direct Transfers | −10·0 | 10·0 | | | | | | |
| 5. Errors and omissions | −1·5 | | 1·0 | | 1·3 | −2·3 | | 1·6 |
| 6. Total Uses | 233·0 | 9·7 | 36·4 | 7·5 | 4·7 | | | |
| 6.1. Investments | 11·2 | 9·7 | 10·5 | 2·0 | 4·7 | | | |
| 6.2. Consumption | 221·8 | | 26·0 | 5·5 | | | | |

*Source:* Summation of the annual tables in the Appendix. Small differences in totals are due to rounding.

would be state banks that mainly utilize their own capital or loans from the Central Bank to make investments. In the total sources of funds for commercial banks, sight deposits (both "commercial" and "savings") account for the largest share (sixty-two per cent in 1959). Their own proprietary resources are as low as eight per cent of the total. Time deposits are very small compared to sight deposits. The placements of the commercial banks are largely short-term loans or discounts. Participations (or investments) are less than three per cent of the total assets and are small (about one-third) even when compared with their own proprietary resources.

The Industrial Development Bank of Turkey is a category in itself, which uses its resources—mainly foreign funds or domestic non-deposit sources—for long-term credits to industry. A very recent addition to this category is a consortium founded by some commercial banks to provide medium-term credits to industry.

With this background information, we can turn to the analysis of fund transfers and resource allocation from 1950 to 1960. A very aggregated picture of the eleven years, based on the financial accounts, is given in Table 7. This shows the eleven-year averages of the sources and uses of funds as percentages of total resources in the economy (percentages computed annually, then averaged).[15] Because these figures are averages, they conceal many interesting developments, some of which we shall examine below.

TABLE 7: SOURCES AND USES OF RESOURCES, 1950–60
(As per cent of total resources)

| | | |
|---|---|---|
| Total real resources | | 100·0 |
| GDP | 97·8 | |
| Import surplus | 2·2 | |
| Public real expenditure | | 16·8 |
| Public investment | 5·5 | |
| Public consumption | 11·3 | |
| Financed by: | | |
| Fiscal transfers | 14·7 | (of which about 0·9% from foreign sources) |
| Monetary transfers | 2·1 | |
| Private real expenditure | | 83·2 |
| Private investment | 7·3 | |
| Private consumption | 75·9 | |
| Financed by: | | |
| Monetary transfers | 1·9 | |
| Directly | 81·3 | |

*Note:* The definitions of fiscal and monetary transfers are located in the Appendix as are the data upon which this table is based. One difference should be noted. Here the level of aggregation of the household sector has been reduced in order to show the growth of bank credit to households for agriculture and house-building as monetary transfers rather than its being cancelled out by the offsetting and greater growth of deposit balances. Thus, the monetary transfers which finance private real expenditure consist here of agricultural and mortgage credits plus the monetary transfers to businesses (change in credits minus change in deposits) which are shown in the annual tables.

First, there is the problem of the significance of monetary transfers in the economy. It is evident from Table 7 that the monetary transfers were important in financing public expenditure and, though to a somewhat lesser extent, did contribute to funds in the private sector as well. Over the decade, the share of monetary transfers in financing of public expenditures, and also as a percentage of the total resources in the economy, grew with the inflation. This, of course, follows from the nature of the mechanism. Monetary transfers became important as inflation gained speed, and, when the increase in money and the rise in prices slowed down, the monetary transfers became less significant. In the six years following 1952, annual transfers of new funds through monetary channels were equal to about six per cent of total resources in the economy. In the three years following the stabilization measures of 1958, this ratio dropped to 2·5 per cent. This shows that unless an inflationary policy is pursued the banking system would be unable to transfer more funds than about two to three per cent of total resources per annum.

The biggest beneficiary of monetary transfers during this period was the state sector. The funds that the state sector secured from the banking system not only increased as a result of the increasing level of total monetary transfers, but the relative distribution of monetary funds among the sectors changed sharply in favour of the state sector, and at the expense of agriculture and private business (Diagram 6). Thus, funds from the banking system became an important element in financing the public expenditure.

The trend of public expenditure and the way it was financed are shown in Diagram 7. Public expenditure during the period varied between 16·5 and 17·5 per cent of the total resources. It showed a slight fall before 1954, then increased until 1957, reaching the 17·5 per cent level in that year. Then there was another slight fall. The main source of finance for public expenditure was, or course, fiscal transfers. These transfers (excluding the foreign component) started from a level of about fifteen per cent of total resources in 1950–51, then there was a significant fall to thirteen per cent by 1954–55, and

DIAGRAM 6: DISTRIBUTION OF MONETARY TRANSFERS

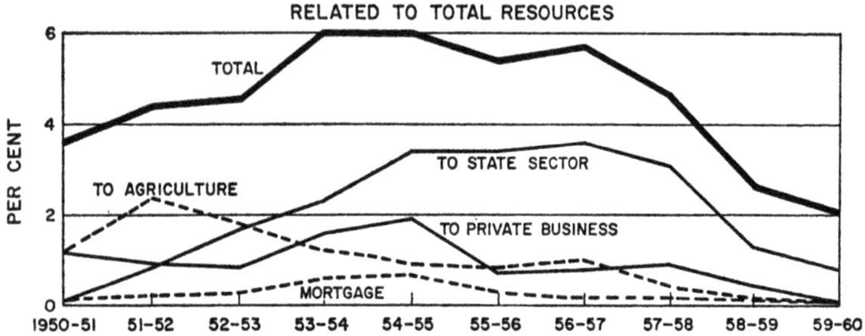


Two-year moving averages. Includes monetary transfers to the business and state sectors (from Annual Tables in Appendix) and bank credits given to agriculture and for mortgages (from *Monthly Bulletin* of the Central Bank).

the level fluctuated around this point after 1955 (Diagram 7). Foreign aid and credit contributed to the budget another financial flow which was equal to about five per cent of public expenditures on the average.

Thus, with public expenditure remaining level or even rising, and with fiscal revenues falling by two percentage points, the gap was covered by monetary transfers. This meant that monetary transfers to the public sector rose and reached significant amounts during 1954–58. In fact, from 1953 to 1958 monetary transfers to the state sector averaged about 3·5 per cent of total resources or about one-fifth of the total public expenditure. It is clear that the magnitude of deficit financing by the government in this period was high.

On the expenditure side, public consumption as a percentage of total resources fell from 13·5 per cent in 1950–51 to about 10·5 per cent in 1954–55. This enabled public investment to rise sharply. The increase in public investment did not stop at that time, but continued until 1956–57. It was realized partly by a slight rise in the share of fiscal transfers and partly by monetary transfers at still higher rates (Diagram 7).

Although large-scale transfers of monetary funds helped to keep the public expenditure ratios from falling in the face of falling fiscal revenues, they could not maintain the total level of both public expenditure and private investment. In the early years of mild inflation, this total as a percentage of total resources rose. But after 1954–55 it started falling due to a sharp drop in the level of private

DIAGRAM 7: PUBLIC EXPENDITURES AND THEIR FINANCING
(As per cent of total resources)

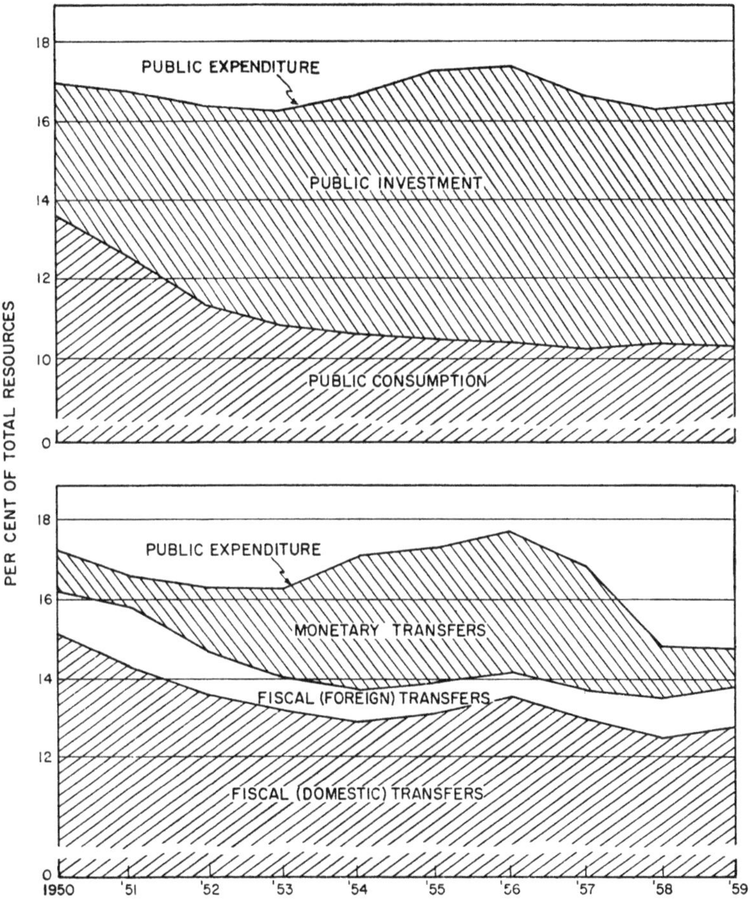


*Source:* Computed from Appendix.

investments. Thus, prior to the stabilization policy of 1958, the private consumption component of the total resources had started rising (Diagram 8).

It is difficult to attribute this fall in the proportion of private investment to a single cause. It could be that too large a part of the resources was being transferred to the state sector. But the fall in private investment was larger than the rise in public expenditure. It would also be expected that shortages due to inflation and controls would have had a negative effect. One of the most important bottlenecks in the economy occurred in imported goods. The trend of private investment runs parallel to the import surplus. In view of the fact that total investment figures in Turkey were based on estimates

DIAGRAM 8: USES OF RESOURCES

(As per cent of total resources)

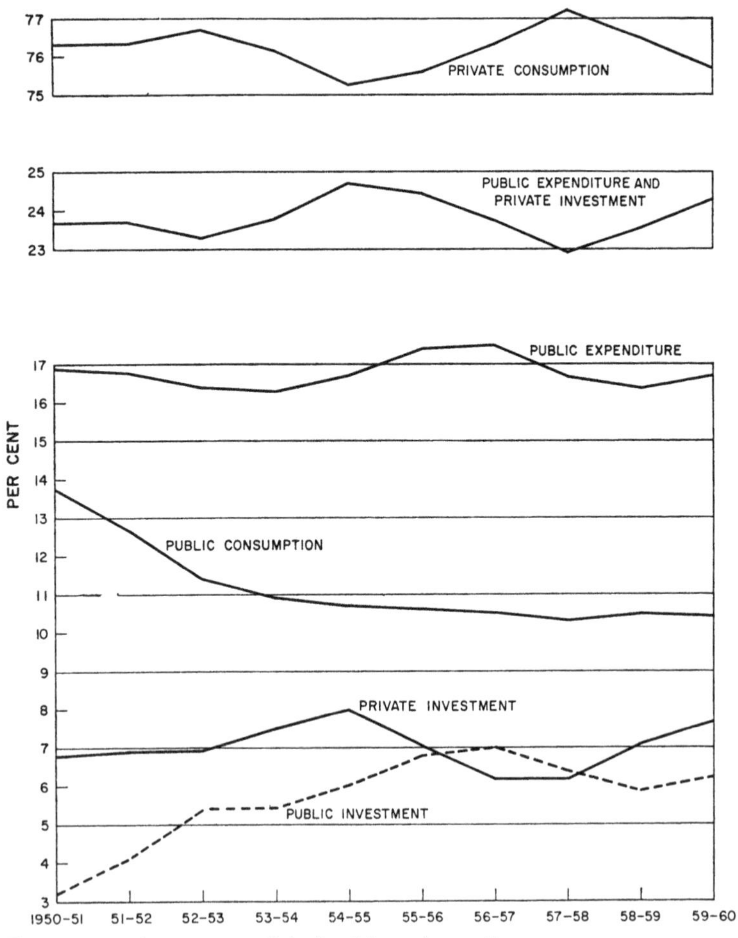


Two-year moving averages. Calculated from Appendix.

of the materials used—the import component of which is quite high—this is not surprising and could be partly explained as a bias in the method of estimation.

Despite all the reservations, one point is clear from this discussion: whether it was due to the shift in monetary transfers in favour of the state sector, to the shortages and bottlenecks that were created, or to the resulting balance-of-payments difficulties, inflationary finance seems to have had a negative effect on the mobilization of resources for development purposes in the economy.

Another interesting generalization suggested by the data is that this period can be neatly divided into three phases. 1950–54 is the slow-inflation period. The money supply rose, but not as rapidly as later, and a buffer was provided by the spectacular increase in real income and foreign aid. It could perhaps be argued that at least a small part of the increase in real income was due to the push of the monetary policy. But after 1954 things take a different turn. The money supply increased more rapidly and the import possibilities shrank. Real income grew very slowly. All sorts of difficulties arose in this atmosphere of rapid inflation, and the share of development expenditure in the use of total resources fell. After the 1958 stabilization policy, the inflation slowed, and most of the indicators indicate that there was a recession.

After having seen the pattern of fund transfers and final uses during 1950–60, it will be interesting to compare this picture of the past with the targets and projections of the Five-Year Plan. For this purpose, the definitions in the Plan were adjusted to obtain figures comparable to the ones we have used in the financial accounts. The comparison of the two sets of data, past and future, may give an idea of the magnitude of the transformation projected in the Five-Year Plan (Diagram 9) and the difficulties policy-makers have had to face to implement such a transformation.

## The Development of the Financial Structure and Economic Growth

All the developments we have discussed so far have had important effects on the stability and growth of the economy. But none of them has necessarily been related to the development of a financial structure which will *in itself* add to the efficiency of the system and not serve simply as an instrument of public expenditure policy. What happened was that the problem of financing development was treated more as a problem in public finance than as a problem in monetary policy. In very simple terms, there was a policy of inflationary finance

DIAGRAM 9: FINANCING PUBLIC EXPENDITURE, PAST AND PLANNED

(As per cent of total resources)

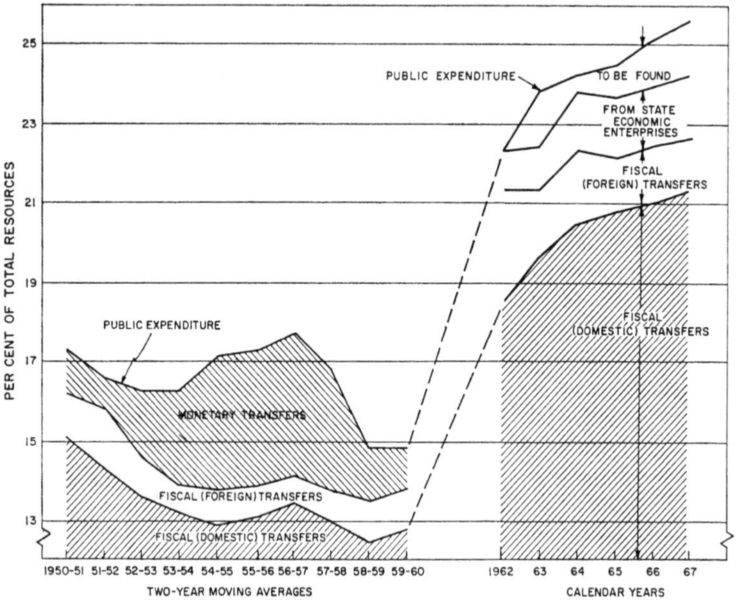


Data up to 1960 are from the Appendix. 1962 is a forecast made in the plan and 1963–67 are the plan targets.

which amounted to the following: Money was produced partly by the Central Bank and partly by other banks as described in the second part of this paper, and the savings which were forced on the economy through this mechanism were spent mostly by the government, as described in the third part. These things, by themselves, did not have much to do with the development of a financial structure. As long as the assets issued by the system offered no new and free alternatives to real-wealth owners, and as long as the liabilities which were granted provided no flexible alternatives to the real-wealth demanders, what took place was, in essence, the taking advantage of a forced transfer rather than the development of a financial market.

Financial development is a process by which a market for indirect claims on real wealth grows. As long as most wealth is held in the form of real assets, the market for them is of necessity an imperfect and rigid one. The simplest case of this is a barter economy, with all the well-known difficulties of executing an exchange. The transition from a barter economy to a money economy is a big improvement that makes possible a greater degree of division of labour and specialization in the economy. The transition from a money economy to what can be termed a "finance economy" is no less important. In the barter economy, the individual can own only tangible assets. In the money economy, a simple financial asset, namely money, is added to the individual's list of assets. In the finance economy, other financial assets such as bonds and shares are added to the spectrum of assets. This state of affairs facilitates the accumulation of savings, the allocation of these savings to the most productive investments, and the best utilization of the existing productive capacity. The reason is simple: These instruments make possible an even greater degree of specialization and division of labour in dealings with capital: Some people save, others invest, and still others manage enterprises in an environment where these components of the social organization are knitted together in a market. Thus, as one author puts it, dynamism is introduced into the static nature of the wealth pattern in underdeveloped countries.[16]

The importance of the development of a financial superstructure as a prerequisite to overall economic development can be exaggerated. The usual interaction is present between the development of a financial superstructure and the accumulation of capital; but this does not provide a definite answer to the crucial issue of where to start to push. A great part of the answer may depend on the level of development. Much can be achieved by laying the foundations of the economy, at whatever cost, in the initial stage of development. But soon comes a stage beyond which a push produces frustration or even chaos. At this level, one of two alternatives seems inevitable. Either the management of productive assets must be assumed by a monopoly—of course a government monopoly—or a market in financial assets must be created.

Let us take the first alternative. In a collectivist economic organization, financial institutions and instruments may not be important. In such a system, productive activities are directed by "physical planning". At times, even the eventual disappearance of money has been predicted. But in the existing collectivist economies, the money economy has survived to solve problems of distribution and consumption, while the bureaucracy of planning has solved investment and production issues. In such a system, in one sense, the wealth structure of the society is activated by the central management. This is why, in some underdeveloped countries, nationalization has introduced some dynamism into an essentially static situation. After this dynamism is introduced, its maintenance without loss of efficiency is, of course, the next question.

On the other hand, in a social organization where the decisions are not centralized, a financial superstructure seems to be essential for growth beyond an initial stage of development. In a society with less than complete planning, the creation of rich pockets of capitalists who will carry on business without a developed financial mechanism, or the assumption by the government of most investment activities and the use of forced savings, are both poor substitutes for resource mobilization and allocation through an adequately developed financial structure.

In a non-collectivist economy, these two alternatives to the development of a financial market are sometimes introduced in such a way as to suggest that they exhaust the range of development strategies. A strategy based on the creation of wealthy individuals who will make investments without any help from a financial market is not likely to succeed for two reasons. First, this kind of unequal distribution of income and wealth is contrary to the aspirations and values of our times. Secondly, even if this were politically feasible, these rich pockets would need a market in which they could deal, or the arrangement would be rigid and possibly inefficient in the long run.

Nor is government action to increase investments with heavy taxation a good substitute. Not only must the margin of income that can be saved be activated, but the whole existing wealth structure must change. Thus, either an unequal income distribution or a heavy taxation policy might increase savings and investments, but neither would necessarily introduce dynamism into the wealth structure. This is why, no matter what the social policy of a society, whether its orientation be *laissez faire*, welfare state, or planning, there is no good alternative to a financial market. The development of a financial superstructure is not incompatible with any of these social policies. But it is incompatible with the desire to curtail private enterprise. Any attempt to curtail private enterprise must go the whole way and abolish private property in productive assets for the sake of consistency. Otherwise, a mixed economy, where most wealth is owned by individuals, but where the state discourages the development of the financial structure by using every financial mechanism to secure public finance, will have the worst of the two worlds.

If these arguments have some validity, Turkish policy was a failure with respect to the creation of a financial superstructure.

Deposits were considered to be money rather than investments, so the increase in financial assets did not provide individuals with any new alternatives for owning wealth. Even after all the efforts, frustrations, sacrifices, and successes of the last ten or twenty years, the investment alternatives open to individuals today are the same as they were one hundred years ago: real estate or private business.

Even without offering new alternatives to the saver, opportunities for the investor could have been improved in what is known as the money market. Funds have become available as a result of an increase in the money supply, which was money the people were willing to hold because of higher prices or higher real income. This opportunity, which was produced by monetary expansion, could have been used to establish a revolving fund which would have provided the credit market with fluidity and flexibility. In other words, the Central Bank and the banking system as a whole could have established a credit market regulated by the Central Bank. As things were, this opportunity was lost.

As a result, the credit market is rigid and imperfect today. A considerable part of the outstanding total credit, as shown in monetary statistics, lacks fluidity; these are the credits which have been allocated according to laws or decrees rather than by market processes. As a natural consequence, credits granted below market rates become frozen and lose their primary function. A considerable portion of the borrowings by state economic enterprises, and some of the agricultural credits, are in this category. In fact, in 1961, all of the short-term credits of the Central Bank to the state sector were converted into treasury bonds of 100-year term and 0·5 per cent interest. In this atmosphere, people responsible for economic policy have become accustomed to think of public, and even of private, financing problems as problems of direct rather than market allocation, and this habit has not been revised—has in fact been enforced—after the transition into a planned economy.

It cannot be denied that it is difficult, in a mixed economy, to draw a definite line between public finance and the capital-credit market. Some of the funds collected in Turkey by the state, through foreign aid, through increases in the money supply, and by cash surpluses in official or semi-official enterprises, could be transferred to the capital-credit market, as was done in some countries in post-war Europe. Or funds could be acquired on the authority of the state from monetary and credit institutions to finance state investments and other expenditures. But merely using financial or monetary channels for public finance could be harmful from the standpoint of the three aspects of finance we have discussed in this chapter. The effect on the price level and the emergence of inflation is a constant danger. When the Central Bank is reduced to a mint or a department of the Treasury, dangers and disadvantages arise on two counts: first, the traditional system of parliamentary control of public revenue is not extended effectively to deficit financing when it is arranged through numerous and obscure channels. In the case of taxation, on the other hand, the cost of capital is discussed on a political platform, and the taxation and budget acts are subject to ratification by the parliament. The cost of capital, and who pays for it, are much clearer. Actually, the characteristic obscurity of monetary transfers is what appeals to the so-called "wizards" of finance. Secondly, when most of the resources of the Central Bank are used to finance public enterprises, there is not much possibility or room left for manoeuvre in monetary policy, so the Central Bank can have little regulating influence on the money market. The Central Bank becomes just an agency producing paper money and exercises no effective control over the system as a whole.

One difference between public and private finance is that public finance involves the compulsory taking of funds, whereas private finance involves voluntary borrowing or participation. To the extent that funds are transferred at interest rates much below the market rate, such transactions move further away from voluntary borrowing and approach compulsory taking. This produces two problems: First, it destroys any control based on a criterion of rational allocation. Who will use the funds is not determined by who bids the highest, but by decisions made across the desks of the bureaucracy. Our position is not that there should be no deviation from the strict economic calculus when reasonably defined cases of high social benefit exist. But even then, even when the return is arbitrarily determined, the cost of the capital must be known, must be paid for, and the parties that actually pay it should be made explicit.

Secondly, financial arrangements which are made at free prices create a market which promotes investment in its own right. Transactions which are forced through at less than market prices do not create such a market and become once-for-all transfers. For example, the debts of the State sector to the Central Bank, amounting to over five billion liras, which were converted in 1961 into 100-year 0·5 per cent interest treasury bonds, and the credits given out by the Agricultural Bank, have created no marketable financial assets except for signed documents in the files.

It is obvious that the rate-of-interest structure is a very important element in any financial structure. In Turkey, due to the undeveloped condition of the market, the rate-of-interest structure is very imperfect. Many funds in the financial sphere are transferred at symbolic rates, while in the market very high interest rates prevail—between fifteen and thirty per cent. The highness of the rates may reflect an inflation premium and not the pure rate. Nevertheless, nowadays when prices are rising at two to four per cent per annum, this leaves pure rates of eleven to twenty-six per cent which are still high. Surely, it is difficult to speak of an interest rate level that is so high without taking into consideration many other aspects of the situation. A rate of twenty per cent is high by any standards, and above the debatable limit. This could be a good thing if there were a demand for funds for stable productive purposes at this rate. It is difficult to see the probability of non-speculative economic investments being able to pay twenty per cent per annum. Nor are these rates available to savers. Due to the imperfections of the credit market, the most that one can have from a financial placement is by having time deposits at six per cent, which after adjustment for expected price increases might be two to four per cent per annum.

Several factors may be responsible for the high rates of interest for freely available credit. A great proportion of the funds in Turkey that could supply the credit market (e.g. social insurance collections, Central Bank credits, and foreign and counterpart loans) are either rationed directly or allocated at very low rates of interest. Privileged rates for certain types of transactions and credit quotas are common. Thus, when the bulk of loanable funds is used up at low average rates of interest, the limited funds remaining are only able to satisfy the needs of emergency and marginal borrowers who can offer high rates for one reason or other, but are not likely to borrow for continuous competitive production.

One implication of the high interest rates for credits, and the low interest rates on deposits, is that banks must be making large profits. Yet this does not seem to be the case. In 1962 the expenses of banks per unit of deposit liabilities were eight per cent for the seven biggest commercial banks. As most of their deposits were sight deposits at two per cent interest, this shows that non-price competition has increased the expense of carrying deposits without giving any direct benefits to the depositors. In fact, the establishment of numerous branch offices not far from each other, and the expense of buildings, furniture, decorative offices, and advertisements, are strong evidence of this. This only shows the waste involved in a banking structure with controlled rates of interest.

The most favourable aspect of the Five-Year Plan, as it was when adopted in 1962, was its negative attitude to an inflationary policy. Paying for public expenditures by deficit financing from the Central Bank was rejected, but even this was not a very dependable stand. As pointed out in the previous section, the public-expenditure and fiscal-transfer targets in the Plan were on the ambitious side. It was doubtful whether a drastic jump in public revenue could be achieved without any monetary transfers (Diagram 9). Although this is not the place to review developments during the First Plan, it is evident from banking statistics that the size of the gap has necessitated some resort to inflationary finance, and even then the planners could not fully achieve the planned investments.

Also, planning may lead to, and the First Plan actually spelled out some steps towards, further regimentation in the credit market. Almost all the foreign, counterpart, and social insurance funds that could be put into a money and capital market are being used to finance public expenditure. Not much is left for creating and feeding a financial market. All these factors indicate that the potentialities of a well-functioning financial superstructure were not fully appreciated in preparing the Turkish Five-Year Plan.

If Turkey is to remain a mixed economy, two institutional reforms are urgently needed. One of these is to co-ordinate banking policy with the needs of a money and credit market. This calls for a very carefully prepared programme which will establish basic principles, and at the same time provide enough funds to implement the reforms. The objective is to create a market which will have flexibility and stability. In order to have flexibility, the role of the interest rate must be re-established. This is a subject which must be investigated from all angles, but at present a lowering of the rate of interest by rediscount policy of the Central Bank could go a long way toward achieving both purposes. This would lower the short-term rate of interest and also give some control to the Central Bank. This does not seem to be in conflict with the principles of the 1958 stabilization policy, which put an end to state borrowing from the Central Bank on a large scale.[17] But some loopholes have been left in the policy, such as the financing of seasonal needs of the Soil Products Office, which was responsible for a good part of the deficit financing and hence of inflation in the past.

These measures may help to create a flexible credit market and, in this way, facilitate financial transactions among the traders and the producers. Although an important step in the right direction, such results will be far from satisfactory in "activating the wealth structure", and in offering alternatives to savers and opportunities to investors. For this, new institutions are necessary and this is a difficult subject in financial organization, because any proposals must take into account the peculiarities of the economy. In view of the recent interest in "promoting capital markets in developing countries", it should be pointed out that the establishment of a stock exchange, and the promotion of the buying of shares by small savers, are not the only, nor—in view of the conditions of the underdeveloped economy—even the most important, steps. All over the world the tendency seems to be toward the development of more institutional channels, the most important one of which is life insurance. But investment banks, investment trusts, *bank d'affairs*, development banks, and corporations are all important institutions to be considered. Once a large enough market is created to make more division of labour possible, these institutions may start specializing in different functions of the financial structure. Saving institutions, promotional institutions, and investment institutions can contribute a great deal to the development efforts of the poor countries which are about to "take off".

## NOTES

1. It should be pointed out that although the contrast in emphasis, particularly in development planning, between the real and the financial aspects of development is sharp, analysis of the financial aspects of development in the recent literature is by no means lacking. For a useful bibliography on the subject see Edward Nevin, *Capital Funds in Underdeveloped Countries*, St. Martin's Press, New York, 1961.

2. Geoffrey Maynard, *Economic Development and the Price Level*, London, 1962. Dudley Seers, "A Theory of Inflation and Growth in Underdeveloped Economies Based on the Experience of Latin America", *Oxford Economic Papers*, June 1942. Joseph Grunwald, "The Structuralist School on Price Stability and Development: The Chilean Case", in *Latin American Issues*, ed. Albert O. Hirshman.

3. United Nations, *Domestic Financing of Economic Development*, 1951, II B, New York, 1950, p. 1.

4. This is perhaps the most underdeveloped chapter in the theory of economic development. For examples of recent attempts in this direction see John Gurley and Edward Shaw, "Financial Aspects of Economic Development," *American Economic Review*, September 1955; Raymond Goldsmith, "Financial Structure and Economic Growth in Advanced Countries", in *Capital Formation and Economic Growth*, Princeton University Press for the National Bureau of Economic Research, Special Conference Series No. 6, 1956.

5. The figures for government bonds in the table are figures net of the bonds held in the portfolio of the banks, except that no deduction could be made for an additional amount of government bonds held by the banks as legal reserves but not separately reported. It is also likely that some of the government bonds are in the hands of government institutions, particularly the Amortization and Credit Fund, an organization responsible for managing the public debt.

6. The large share of the banking system in the financial structure seems to be typical of economies at the early stages of development. Raymond Goldsmith says, "Before the Industrial Revolution, intangibles took the form predominantly of loans among individuals, unincorporated business enterprises and governments. Financial intermediaries were almost entirely absent. The first intermediaries to acquire substantial importance—measured by their assets in comparison with national assets—were banks of issue. Commercial banks (banks of deposit) followed. In the first century after the Industrial Revolution—i.e. in Western Europe and North America until approximately the middle of the nineteenth century—financial intermediaries other than banks remained small and played only a subsidiary role in the financial structure . . . . Since statistics have been available, i.e. since late in the nineteenth century, the share of the banking system in national assets and its contribution to the financial interrelations ratio had a tendency to decline." *Op. cit.*, p. 159.

7. Committee on Finance and Industry, *Report* (Macmillan Committee Report), Her Majesty's Stationery Office, London, 1931, pp. 12–13.

8. This is quite different from the general usage of the terms commercial and savings deposits. The usual meanings are that the first are sight (demand) deposits subject to check and the second are time deposits. To avoid misunderstanding, "commercial deposits" and "saving deposits" will be written hereafter in quotation marks to signify the Turkish usage.

9. For the derivation of the equation see Milton Friedman and Anna Schwartz,

*A Monetary History of the United States 1867–1960*, Princeton University Press, 1963, Appendix B.

10. According to the original Central Bank Act of 1930, the powers of the bank to increase the note issue and to advance credits to the state were quite limited. The Central Bank Act was supposed to be followed by a Stabilization Act, which would determine the principles of note issue and the gold backing of the Turkish lira. In view of the failure of attempts to return to gold all over the world in the early thirties, this second law was never enacted. Instead, the power of the Central Bank to increase the circulation of bank notes by advancing credits was increased. An amendment in 1932 enabled the Treasury to borrow more freely and an amendment in 1938 empowered the Bank to extend credits to the State Economic Enterprises on their Treasury-guaranteed bonds.

11. "Until the Stabilization Act is put into effect, the total of bank notes which the Bank may issue against the operations listed under paragraphs 1, 2, and 4 of article 38, shall be restricted to an amount to be agreed upon by a committee comprising the representatives of the banks whose paid-up capital is not less than four million Turkish liras." Article 39 of the Central Bank Act.

12. All through the analysis of the money supply, deposits at the Central Bank are not taken into account due to the difficulty of classifying these deposits into components relevant for our purposes. In particular, there is a wide discrepancy in the figures from different sources for the portion of these deposits that belong to other banks. For example, at the end of 1962, this amount, according to the Central Bank's balance sheet, is 639 million liras, but it is 252 million liras according to the consolidated balance sheet of the banks which is reported in the same bulletin of the Central Bank. Since the magnitude of unblocked deposits at the Central Bank is not large, and since a high proportion—e.g. the official deposits—would have to be subtracted anyhow in arriving at a money supply figure, this omission will not significantly affect our analysis.

13. An interesting shift in the functional relationship between the two ratios apparently occurred around 1945. Prior to that date, changes in one ratio were accompanied by approximately equal changes in the other. But after that date, the response of the "commercial deposits"-currency ratio was dampened. It even turned downward after 1955. Whether "commercial deposits" were becoming less desirable because of changes in interest rate differentials, opportunities for tax evasion, or some other factors, we do not know. However, we consider the substitutability of one for the other from the standpoint of depositors to have remained high enough to warrant the inclusion of both in our definition of money.

14. In our model, the free deposit balances of the commercial banks at the Central Bank should be included in the definition of "high-powered" money, which has so far been limited to the currency issue, and also in the definition of reserves of the banks. Because of statistical difficulties, currency in circulation (bank notes and coins) is taken as an approximation to the total "high-powered" money and the vault cash of the banks is taken as an approximation to the total free reserves (excluding interbank deposits) of the banks.

15. The total resources figure is used as a denominator for percentage calculations here and later in the paper so as to bring out the allocation relationships and to render them comparable over time.

16. Anders Östlind in *Scope for Non-inflationary Economic Expansion in Turkey*, State Planning Organization, May 1962 (mimeographed). The analysis in this section of the paper has benefited a great deal from Mr. Östlind's study.

17. Surprisingly, this argument is not in conflict with the view that interest rates in Turkey should be raised either. The difference is in the time periods considered. In the short term, when supply is taken as given, a high rate of interest which will equate funds supplied and demanded is better than a below-equilibrium rate which calls for credit rationing. In the longer run, the supply should be increased by letting more real savings go through the organized market so that the equilibrium market rate of interest may settle within a reasonable range.

## *APPENDIX TO CHAPTER 5: FINANCIAL ACCOUNTS*

### *Structure of the Financial Accounts*

In the tables which follow, each column stands for an institutional sector. The entries in a column are arranged according to the following equation: resources+fiscal transfers+monetary transfers +direct transfers+errors and omissions = uses. The real resources which are made available to the economy by the originating sectors are shown in the top section, the financial transfers which effect their ultimate distribution are shown in the middle sections and their distribution among final uses is shown in the bottom section. The algebraic sum of transfers and of errors and omissions is zero row by row. Transfers received by sectors are plus figures and transfers paid are minus figures.

Lack of data has forced certain simplifying assumptions which depart from the conventional national income accounting definitions with respect to (*a*) the sectors to which resources, flows and expenditures are attributed, and (*b*) the categories of transfers identified. These simplifying assumptions are summarized below.

### *Sectors*

The *household* sector provides all the gross domestic product; makes all tax and other domestic revenue payments to the government except corporation tax and production tax; owns all "saving deposits"; receives all agricultural and mortgage credits; and makes all investments in non-industrial and non-commercial buildings.

The *business* sector pays the corporation tax and the production tax; owns all "commercial deposits"; receives all commercial credits; makes all private investments except those in private buildings (which are under household); and receives capital directly from households for investment.

The *central government* sector makes expenditures covered by the central and annexed budgets and finances them.

The *local government* sector makes expenditures covered by the budgets of municipalities and "special administrations" and finances them.

The *state economic enterprises* sector makes all state investments which are not shown under the central or local government sectors and finances them.

The *rest of the world* sector provides the import surplus; gives loans and grants and receives debt service.

The *banks* sector is an intermediary sector whose four types of financial institutions may each gain or lose funds but together always have zero receipts.

The *undistributable* sector collects items from the balance sheets of financial institutions which could not be identified by sector.

### *Transfers*

Transfers are the changes in the immediate command over resources among the sectors. Conceptually, three kinds of transfers could be distinguished: compulsory taking by the government as in the case of taxation; fixed-return credit transactions between lenders and borrowers; and variable-return direct transfers between savers and investors. A more institutional classification is used in the following tables where the fiscal transfers include all the transactions that go through the budgets except the finance of the public sector by the banking system which is taken into account in the monetary transfers. Similarly, all the transactions in which banks deal are analysed in monetary transfers. Thus these include some non-credit transactions as well. Finally, all the resources of the household sector that remain after consumption and investment in housing have been deducted are assumed to be transferred directly to the business sector. These may range from investments in actual stocks to private credit transactions, or may even be just two aspects of the behaviour of the same person—as income earner and as entrepreneur.

The fiscal transfers are sub-classified according to the kinds of flows, whereas the monetary transfers are sub-classified according to the institutions. As indicated in the notes on sources below, the fiscal transfers are calculated from the budget accounts by attributing receipts and disbursements to the other sectors. The monetary transfers are calculated from the differences in year-to-year balance-sheet values of the financial intermediaries. The direct transfers are residuals.

### *Errors and omissions*

The accounts of the household sector and the business sector are open-ended in the sense that a residual item secures that the sources and uses of funds balance through that residual item—in the case of households, consumption, and in the case of businesses, the direct transfers. Local government accounts balance without the help of any residual. But since the central government, state economic enterprises, rest-of-the-world and undistributable columns do not have such adjustment accounts, there occurs a difference between the sources and uses of funds which are estimated independently. In order to show these discrepancies, but at the same time secure consistency, the net result of these differences is closed into the household sector which is kept in balance by an adjustment of consumption as a residual item.

## 1950

(Million current TL)

| | *House-hold* | *Busi-ness* | *Cen-tral Govt.* | *Local Govt.* | *State Eco-nomic Enter.* | *Rest of World* | *Banks* | *Un dis tribu abl* |
|---|---|---|---|---|---|---|---|---|
| 1. Resources | | | | | | | | |
| 1.1. GDP | 10·405 | | | | | | | |
| 1.2. Import Surplus | | | | | | 212 | | |
| TOTAL RESOURCES | 10·405 | | | | | 212 | | |
| 2. Fiscal Transfers | | | | | | | | |
| 2.1. Taxes | −1·340 | −64 | 1·242 | 218 | −56 | | | |
| 2.2. Other Revenue | −428 | | 517 | | | −89 | | |
| 2.3. Budget Transfers | 187 | | −259 | 2 | 60 | 10 | | |
| TOTAL FISCAL TRANS. | −1·581 | −64 | 1·500 | 220 | 4 | −79 | | |
| 3. Monetary Transfers | | | | | | | | |
| 3.1. Central Bank | −59 | | 27 | | 147 | −210 | 94 | |
| 3.2. State Banks | −7 | 44 | 18 | 5 | 15 | | −180 | 1 |
| 3.3. Comm. Banks | −47 | −27 | 25 | | | 64 | −13 | − |
| 3.4. Other Inst. | −36 | −5 | −39 | | −5 | | 99 | −1 |
| TOTAL MONETARY TRANS. | −149 | 12 | 31 | 5 | 157 | −146 | 0 | 9 |
| 4. Direct Transfers | −444 | 444 | | | | | | |
| 5. Errors and omissions | 179 | | −22 | | −80 | 13 | | −9 |
| 6. Total Uses | 8·410 | 392 | 1·509 | 225 | 81 | | | |
| 6.1. Investments | 365 | 392 | 183 | 43 | 81 | | | |
| 6.2. Consumption | 8·045 | | 1·326 | 182 | | | | |

## 1951

(Million current TL)

| | *House-hold* | *Busi-ness* | *Cen-tral Govt.* | *Local Govt.* | *State Eco-nomic Enter.* | *Rest of World* | *Banks* | *Un-dis-tribut-able* |
|---|---|---|---|---|---|---|---|---|
| Resources | | | | | | | | |
| 1.1. GDP | 12·295 | | | | | | | |
| 1.2. Import Surplus | | | | | | 279 | | |
| TOTAL RESOURCES | 12·295 | | | | | 279 | | |
| Fiscal Transfers | | | | | | | | |
| 2.1. Taxes | −1·334 | −74 | 1·237 | 242 | −71 | | | |
| 2.2. Other Revenue | −585 | | 783 | | | −198 | | |
| 2.3. Budget Transfers | 134 | | −235 | 4 | 82 | 15 | | |
| TOTAL FISCAL TRANS. | −1·785 | −74 | 1·785 | 246 | 11 | −183 | | |
| Monetary Transfers | | | | | | | | |
| 3.1. Central Bank | −145 | | 35 | | 171 | 3 | −8 | −56 |
| 3.2. State Banks | 277 | 72 | −101 | 19 | 10 | | −57 | −220 |
| 3.3. Comm. Banks | −111 | 69 | −26 | | | −15 | 97 | −14 |
| 3.4. Other Inst. | −34 | −7 | −40 | | −7 | | −32 | 120 |
| TOTAL MONETARY TRANS. | −13 | 134 | −132 | 19 | 174 | −12 | 0 | −170 |
| Direct Transfers | −374 | 374 | | | | | | |
| Errors and omissions | −84 | | 73 | | −75 | −84 | | 170 |
| Total Uses | 10·039 | 434 | 1·726 | 265 | 110 | | | |
| 6.1. Investment | 376 | 434 | 279 | 56 | 110 | | | |
| 6.2. Consumption | 9·663 | | 1·447 | 209 | | | | |

## 1952

(Million current TL)

| | *House-hold* | *Busi-ness* | *Cen-tral Govt.* | *Local Govt.* | *State Eco-nomic Enter.* | *Rest of World* | *Banks* | *Un-dis-tribu-abl* |
|---|---|---|---|---|---|---|---|---|
| 1. Resources | | | | | | | | |
| 1.1. GDP | 14·352 | | | | | | | |
| 1.2. Import Surplus | | | | | | 558 | | |
| TOTAL RESOURCES | 14·352 | | | | | 558 | | |
| 2. Fiscal Transfers | | | | | | | | |
| 2.1. Taxes | −1·646 | −96 | 1·580 | 268 | −106 | | | |
| 2.2. Other Revenue | −756 | | 994 | | | −238 | | |
| 2.3. Budget Transfers | 443 | | −549 | 37 | 52 | 17 | | |
| TOTAL FISCAL TRANS. | −1·959 | −96 | 2·025 | 305 | −54 | −221 | | |
| 3. Monetary Transfers | | | | | | | | |
| 3.1. Central Bank | −97 | | −35 | | 282 | −240 | 164 | −7 |
| 3.2. State Banks | 371 | 34 | −47 | 29 | 7 | | −323 | −7 |
| 3.3. Comm. Banks | −111 | 98 | −14 | | | −16 | 53 | −1 |
| 3.4. Other Inst. | −26 | −12 | −40 | | −12 | | 106 | −1 |
| TOTAL MONETARY TRANS. | 137 | 120 | −136 | 29 | 277 | −256 | 0 | −17 |
| 4. Direct Transfers | −579 | 579 | | | | | | |
| 5. Errors and omissions | −158 | | 149 | | −81 | −81 | | 17 |
| 6. Total Uses | 11·793 | 603 | 2·038 | 334 | 142 | | | |
| 6.1. Investments | 506 | 603 | 460 | 93 | 142 | | | |
| 6.2. Consumption | 11·287 | | 1·578 | 241 | | | | |

## 1953

(Million current TL)

| | *House-hold* | *Busi-ness* | *Cen-tral Govt.* | *Local Govt.* | *State Eco-nomic Enter.* | *Rest of World* | *Banks* | *Un-dis-tribut-able* |
|---|---|---|---|---|---|---|---|---|
| Resources | | | | | | | | |
| 1.1. GDP | 16·851 | | | | | | | |
| 1.2. Import Surplus | | | | | | 462 | | |
| TOTAL RESOURCES | 16·851 | | | | | 462 | | |
| Fiscal Transfers | | | | | | | | |
| 2.1. Taxes | −1·924 | −118 | 1·853 | 307 | −118 | | | |
| 2.2 Other Revenue | −397 | | 512 | | | −115 | | |
| 2.3. Budget Transfers | 93 | | −297 | 43 | 130 | 31 | | |
| TOTAL FISCAL TRANS. | −2·228 | −118 | 2·068 | 350 | 12 | −84 | | |
| Monetary Transfers | | | | | | | | |
| 3.1. Central Bank | −182 | | −21 | | 222 | 108 | 56 | −183 |
| 3.2. State Banks | 47 | 26 | 53 | 53 | 145 | | −167 | −157 |
| 3.3. Comm. Banks | −180 | 117 | 13 | | | −25 | 44 | 31 |
| 3.4. Other Inst. | −3 | −9 | −36 | | −9 | | 67 | −10 |
| TOTAL MONETARY TRANS. | −318 | 134 | 9 | 53 | 358 | 83 | 0 | −319 |
| Direct Transfers | −535 | 535 | | | | | | |
| Errors and omissions | 235 | | −23 | | −70 | −461 | | 319 |
| Total Uses | 14·005 | 551 | 2·054 | 403 | 300 | | | |
| 5.1. Investments | 568 | 551 | 508 | 113 | 300 | | | |
| 5.2. Consumption | 13·437 | | 1·546 | 290 | | | | |

**1954**

(Million current TL)

| | House-hold | Busi-ness | Cen-tral Govt. | Local Govt. | State Eco-nomic Enter. | Rest of World | Banks | U di trib ab |
|---|---|---|---|---|---|---|---|---|
| 1. Resources | | | | | | | | |
| 1.1. GDP | 17·159 | | | | | | | |
| 1.2. Import Surplus | | | | | | 499 | | |
| TOTAL RESOURCES | 17·159 | | | | | 499 | | |
| 2. Fiscal Transfers | | | | | | | | |
| 2.1. Taxes | −2·157 | −139 | 2·094 | 331 | −129 | | | |
| 2.2. Other Revenue | −206 | | 393 | | | −187 | | |
| 2.3. Budget Transfers | 220 | | −372 | 41 | 75 | 36 | | |
| TOTAL FISCAL TRANS. | −2·143 | −139 | 2·115 | 372 | −54 | −151 | | |
| 3. Monetary Transfers | | | | | | | | |
| 3.1. Central Bank | −40 | | 197 | | 130 | −451 | 541 | −3 |
| 3.2. State Banks | 205 | 271 | −53 | 65 | 156 | | −446 | −1 |
| 3.3. Comm. Banks | −211 | 270 | −10 | | | −43 | 75 | — |
| 3.4. Other Inst. | −5 | −15 | −57 | | −15 | | −170 | 2 |
| TOTAL MONETARY TRANS. | −51 | 526 | 77 | 65 | 271 | −494 | 0 | −3 |
| 4. Direct Transfers | −279 | 279 | | | | | | |
| 5. Errors and omissions | −641 | | 41 | | 60 | 146 | | 3 |
| 6. Total Uses | 14·045 | 666 | 2·233 | 437 | 277 | | | |
| 6.1. Investments | 844 | 666 | 567 | 120 | 277 | | | |
| 6.2. Consumption | 13·201 | | 1·666 | 317 | | | | |

## 1955

(Million current TL)

| | *House-hold* | *Busi-ness* | *Cen-tral Govt.* | *Local Govt.* | *State Eco-nomic Enter.* | *Rest of World* | *Banks* | *Un-dis-tribut-able* |
|---|---|---|---|---|---|---|---|---|
| Resources | | | | | | | | |
| 1.1. GDP | 21·133 | | | | | | | |
| 1.2. Import Surplus | | | | | | 499 | | |
| TOTAL RESOURCES | 21·133 | | | | | 499 | | |
| Fiscal Transfers | | | | | | | | |
| 2.1. Taxes | −2·572 | −193 | 2·482 | 415 | −132 | | | |
| 2.2. Other Revenue | −213 | | 412 | | | −199 | | |
| 2.3. Budget Transfers | 192 | | −387 | 46 | 114 | 35 | | |
| TOTAL FISCAL TRANS. | −2·593 | −193 | 2·507 | 461 | −18 | −164 | | |
| Monetary Transfers | | | | | | | | |
| 3.1. Central Bank | −418 | | 177 | | 206 | −125 | −193 | 353 |
| 3.2. State Banks | 33 | 67 | −65 | 37 | 349 | | −411 | −10 |
| 3.3. Comm. Banks | −209 | 157 | −13 | | 355 | −17 | 407 | −680 |
| 3.4. Other Inst. | −19 | −21 | −59 | | −21 | | 197 | −77 |
| TOTAL MONETARY TRANS. | −613 | 203 | 40 | 37 | 889 | −142 | 0 | −414 |
| Direct Transfers | −546 | 546 | | | | | | |
| Errors and omissions | 60 | | 62 | | −343 | −193 | | 414 |
| Total Uses | 17·441 | 556 | 2·609 | 498 | 528 | | | |
| 6.1. Investments | 1·064 | 556 | 727 | 147 | 528 | | | |
| 6.2. Consumption | 16·377 | | 1·882 | 351 | | | | |

## 1956

(Million current TL)

| | House-hold | Busi-ness | Cen-tral Govt. | Local Govt. | State Eco-nomic Enter. | Rest of World | Banks | Un-dis-tribu-abl… |
|---|---|---|---|---|---|---|---|---|
| 1. Resources | | | | | | | | |
| 1.1. GDP | 24·431 | | | | | | | |
| 1.2. Import Surplus | | | | | | 212 | | |
| TOTAL RESOURCES | 24·431 | | | | | 212 | | |
| 2. Fiscal Transfers | | | | | | | | |
| 2.1. Taxes | −2·828 | −241 | 2·815 | 455 | −201 | | | |
| 2.2. Other Revenue | −445 | | 699 | | | −254 | | |
| 2.3. Budget Transfers | 206 | | —375 | 54 | 73 | 42 | | |
| TOTAL FISCAL TRANS. | −3·067 | −241 | 3·139 | 509 | −128 | −212 | | |
| 3. Monetary Transfers | | | | | | | | |
| 3.1. Central Bank | −509 | | 276 | | −81 | 9 | 261 | [illegible] |
| 3.2. State Banks | 212 | 50 | −7 | 64 | 385 | | −500 | −2[illegible] |
| 3.3. Comm. Banks | −390 | 117 | 18 | | | −27 | 193 | [illegible] |
| 3.4. Other Inst. | −7 | −26 | −64 | | −26 | | 46 | [illegible] |
| TOTAL MONETARY TRANS. | −694 | 141 | 223 | 64 | 278 | −18 | 0 | |
| 4. Direct Transfers | −615 | 615 | | | | | | |
| 5. Errors and omissions | −366 | | −105 | | 459 | 18 | | −[illegible] |
| 6. Total Uses | 19·689 | 515 | 3·257 | 573 | 609 | | | |
| 6.1. Investments | 1·108 | 515 | 966 | 168 | 609 | | | |
| 6.2. Consumption | 18·581 | | 2·291 | 405 | | | | |

## 1957

(Million current TL)

| | *House-hold* | *Busi-ness* | *Cen-tral Govt.* | *Local Govt.* | *State Eco-nomic Enter.* | *Rest of World* | *Banks* | *Un-dis-tribut-able* |
|---|---|---|---|---|---|---|---|---|
| Resources | | | | | | | | |
| 1.1. GDP | 30·668 | | | | | | | |
| 1.2. Import Surplus | | | | | | 253 | | |
| TOTAL RESOURCES | 30·668 | | | | | 253 | | |
| Fiscal Transfers | | | | | | | | |
| 2.1. Taxes | −3·546 | −285 | 3·271 | 758 | −198 | | | |
| 2.2. Other Revenue | −677 | | 835 | | | −158 | | |
| 2.3. Budget Transfers | 313 | | −517 | 51 | 105 | 48 | | |
| TOTAL FISCAL TRANS. | −3·910 | −285 | 3·589 | 809 | −93 | −110 | | |
| Monetary Transfers | | | | | | | | |
| 3.1. Central Bank | −600 | | 129 | | 578 | −271 | 350 | −186 |
| 3.2. State Banks | −130 | −35 | 220 | 96 | 596 | | −551 | −196 |
| 3.3. Comm. Banks | −479 | 423 | 13 | | | −15 | 20 | 38 |
| 3.4. Other Inst. | −31 | −40 | −69 | | −40 | | 181 | −1 |
| TOTAL MONETARY TRANS. | −1·240 | 348 | 293 | 96 | 1·134 | −286 | 0 | −345 |
| Direct Transfers | −532 | 532 | | | | | | |
| Errors and omissions | 146 | | −166 | | −468 | 143 | | 345 |
| Total Uses | 25·132 | 595 | 3·716 | 905 | 573 | | | |
| 6.1. Investments | 1·277 | 595 | 1·241 | 237 | 573 | | | |
| 6.2. Consumption | 23·855 | | 2·475 | 668 | | | | |

**1958**

(Million current TL)

| | *House-hold* | *Busi-ness* | *Cen-tral Govt.* | *Local Govt.* | *State Eco-nomic Enter.* | *Rest of World* | *Banks* | *Un dis-tribu-abl* |
|---|---|---|---|---|---|---|---|---|
| 1. Resources | | | | | | | | |
| 1.1. GDP | 38·652 | | | | | | | |
| 1.2. Import Surplus | | | | | | 577 | | |
| TOTAL RESOURCES | 38·652 | | | | | 577 | | |
| 2. Fiscal Transfers | | | | | | | | |
| 2.1. Taxes | −4·294 | −316 | 3·869 | 990 | −249 | | | |
| 2.2. Other Revenue | −580 | | 1·013 | | | −433 | | |
| 2.3. Budget Transfers | 332 | | −540 | 73 | 92 | 43 | | |
| TOTAL FISCAL TRANS. | −4·542 | −316 | 4·342 | 1·063 | −157 | −390 | | |
| 3. Monetary Transfers | | | | | | | | |
| 3.1. Central Bank | −102 | | −21 | | 330 | 249 | 241 | −69 |
| 3.2. State Banks | −52 | 306 | −195 | 175 | 328 | | −439 | −12 |
| 3.3. Comm. Banks | −210 | 25 | 60 | | | 19 | 134 | −2 |
| 3.4. Other Inst. | −47 | −57 | −77 | | −57 | | 64 | 17 |
| TOTAL MONETARY TRANS. | −411 | 274 | −233 | 175 | 601 | 268 | 0 | −67 |
| 4. Direct Transfers | −1·149 | 1·149 | | | | | | |
| 5. Errors and omissions | −844 | | 486 | | 139 | −455 | | 67 |
| 6. Total Uses | 31·706 | 1·107 | 4·595 | 1·238 | 583 | | | |
| 6.1. Investments | 1·487 | 1·107 | 1·412 | 315 | 583 | | | |
| 6.2. Consumption | 30·219 | | 3·183 | 923 | | | | |

## 1959

(Million current TL)

| | *Household* | *Business* | *Central Govt.* | *Local Govt.* | *State Economic Enter.* | *Rest of World* | *Banks* | *Undistributable* |
|---|---|---|---|---|---|---|---|---|
| Resources | | | | | | | | |
| 1.1. GDP | 47·980 | | | | | | | |
| 1.2. Import Surplus | | | | | | 1·308 | | |
| TOTAL RESOURCES | 47·980 | | | | | 1·308 | | |
| Fiscal Transfers | | | | | | | | |
| 2.1. Taxes | −5·643 | −365 | 5·376 | 981 | −349 | | | |
| 2.2. Other Revenue | −637 | | 1·228 | | | −591 | | |
| 2.3. Budget Transfers | 365 | | −671 | 101 | 96 | 109 | | |
| TOTAL FISCAL TRANS. | −5·915 | −365 | 5·933 | 1·082 | −253 | −482 | | |
| Monetary Transfers | | | | | | | | |
| 3.1. Central Bank | −340 | | 135 | | 254 | −251 | −187 | 389 |
| 3.2. State Banks | −68 | −206 | −264 | 188 | 558 | | −267 | 59 |
| 3.3. Comm. Banks | −420 | 399 | 30 | | | −151 | 187 | −45 |
| 3.4. Other Inst. | −105 | −77 | −170 | | −77 | | 267 | 162 |
| TOTAL MONETARY TRANS. | −933 | 116 | −269 | 188 | 735 | −402 | 0 | 565 |
| Direct Transfers | −2·244 | 2·244 | | | | | | |
| Errors and omissions | 309 | | 441 | | 239 | −424 | | −565 |
| Total Uses | 39·197 | 1·995 | 6·105 | 1·270 | 721 | | | |
| 6.1. Investments | 1·733 | 1·995 | 1·895 | 348 | 721 | | | |
| 6.2. Consumption | 37·464 | | 4·210 | 922 | | | | |

## 1960

(Million current TL)

| | House-hold | Busi-ness | Cen-tral Govt. | Local Govt. | State Eco-nomic Enter. | Rest of World | Banks | U[illegible] di[illegible] trib[illegible] ab[illegible] |
|---|---|---|---|---|---|---|---|---|
| 1. Resources | | | | | | | | |
| 1.1. GDP | 51·282 | | | | | | | |
| 1.2. Import Surplus | | | | | | 1·257 | | |
| TOTAL RESOURCES | 51·282 | | | | | 1·257 | | |
| 2. Fiscal Transfers | | | | | | | | |
| 2.1. Taxes | −5·797 | −418 | 5·540 | 1·096 | −421 | | | |
| 2.2. Other Revenue | −792 | | 1·526 | | | −734 | | |
| 2.3. Budget Transfers | 251 | | −664 | 176 | 65 | 172 | | |
| TOTAL FISCAL TRANS. | −6·338 | −418 | 6·402 | 1·272 | −356 | −562 | | |
| 3. Monetary Transfers | | | | | | | | |
| 3.1. Central Bank | −404 | | 618 | | −465 | 42 | −368 | 5 |
| 3.2. State Banks | 188 | 144 | −277 | 92 | 205 | | 181 | −5 |
| 3.3. Comm. Banks | —39 | −98 | 3 | | | 173 | 64 | −1 |
| 3.4. Other Inst. | −108 | −82 | −187 | | −82 | | 123 | 3 |
| TOTAL MONETARY TRANS. | −363 | −36 | 190 | 92 | −342 | 215 | 0 | 2 |
| 4. Direct Transfers | −2·721 | 2·721 | | | | | | |
| 5. Errors and omissions | −360 | | 10 | | 1·504 | −910 | | −2 |
| 6. Total Uses | 41·500 | 2·267 | 6·602 | 1·364 | 806 | | | |
| 6.1. Investments | 1·830 | 2·267 | 2·224 | 379 | 806 | | | |
| 6.2. Consumption | 39·670 | | 4·378 | 985 | | | | |

*Sources:*

Line 1.1: Official estimates of the State Institute of Statistics, Ankara. Last two years preliminary.

Line 1.2: For 1950–51, *International Financial Statistics*. For 1952–62, official Turkish estimates from Agency for International Development, *Turkish Economic Statistics, 1963*, Ankara. (Ed. note: The import data used by Yenal and Shorter in their respective chapters differ in certain respects which may be noted here. Yenal has kept to the orthodox "civilian import surplus" concept, whereas Shorter has introduced an additional component of direct military deliveries. For estimates of the "civilian import surplus", Yenal has relied upon unadjusted official Turkish data, whereas Shorter has employed the balance-of-payments data published by the International Monetary Fund after certain adjustments by the Fund. There are serious deficiencies in the estimates from both sources for the early years in any case. It also turns out that at the level of generality used by Yenal in his analysis, it would not be worth while to make the IMF adjustments to his import data. Indeed, his position, with which the editor fully agrees, is that the degree of accuracy in the present data will support only very limited statements concerning magnitudes, trends, and relationships. Should better data become available in the future, further development of the analysis would then be warranted).

Lines 2.1–2.3: Central government budgets; revenue estimates of local governments in S.I.S., *Statistical Annual*; special data reclassifications prepared by the State Planning Organization; and budget justification bills.

Lines 3.1–3.4: Net annual flows of funds estimated from differences between beginning and end-of-year figures in balance sheet accounts of the financial institutions. Central Bank *Monthly Bulletins*.

Line 4: Calculated as the difference between uses and transfers in the business sector column.

Line 5: Calculated as the difference between uses and transfers recorded in the columns for central government, state economic enterprises, rest of the world, and undistributable. The sum of these differences was entered with an opposite sign as the errors and omissions for households. Zero assumed for other sectors.

Line 6.1: For total investment and household investment, K. Gürtan's estimates were accepted. For the central government, a compilation by the State Planning Organization which adjusts the budget accounts for debt repayments that should be excluded. For local government, an S.P.O. analysis of expenditures. For business, calculated as the difference between the components just specified and the total estimated by K. Gürtan.

Line 6.2: For households, calculated as a residual in the column. For central and local governments, budgets and expenditure data classified by the S.P.O.

For Product Safety Concerns and Information please contact our EU representative GPSR@taylorandfrancis.com
Taylor & Francis Verlag GmbH, Kaufingerstraße 24, 80331 München, Germany

www.ingramcontent.com/pod-product-compliance
Ingram Content Group UK Ltd.
Pitfield, Milton Keynes, MK11 3LW, UK
UKHW021954180926
475701UK00003B/24
*9781138974609*